COLERIDGE & WORDSWORTH
IN THE WEST COUNTRY

Tom Mayberry

with a foreword by
The Lord Coleridge

With best wishes

Tom Mayberry

21 November, 2006

ALAN SUTTON

First published in the United Kingdom in 1992 by
Alan Sutton Publishing Limited · Phoenix Mill · Far Thrupp
Stroud · Gloucestershire

First published in the United States of America in 1992 by
Alan Sutton Publishing Inc · Wolfeboro Falls · NH 03896-0848

British Library Cataloguing in Publication Data

Mayberry, Tom
  Coleridge and Wordsworth in the west country.
  I. Title
  821.7

  ISBN 0–86299–896–4

Library of Congress Cataloging in Publication Data applied for

Typeset in 10/12 Bembo
Typesetting and origination by
Alan Sutton Publishing Limited.
Printed in Great Britain by
The Bath Press Ltd., Avon.

For my Mother and Father

The waterfall in Holford Glen, photographed *c.* 1880. During 1797–8, Coleridge and Wordsworth returned repeatedly to the 'loud Waterfall', which came to represent for them nature's animating presence at the heart of their Quantock lives

CONTENTS

Flowers are lovely; Love is flower-like;
Friendship is a sheltering tree;
O! the joys, that came down shower-like,
Of Friendship, Love, and Liberty,
                    Ere I was old!

From 'Youth and Age'
S.T. Coleridge, 1834

FOREWORD

It is over two hundred years since Samuel Taylor Coleridge, at the age of nine, left Ottery St Mary to begin his school career at Christ's Hospital in London. He seldom returned to his home, and was there for the last time in 1799; but the West Country, like his Devon accent, was part of him until he died. His greatest achievements as a poet, as this book records, will always be associated with Devon and Somerset, and it was during one remarkable year in the Quantock Hills that his friendship with William and Dorothy Wordsworth was firmly established. Though the happy days of their friendship did not last, Wordsworth never forgot his debt to the younger man, and in 1841, seven years after Coleridge's death, paid his only visit to Ottery to see the place he had so often heard described, and to visit the church where Coleridge's beloved father was buried. Tom Mayberry, in his new book, tells us all these things, and more besides, and has discovered many fine illustrations to show us the West Country world the poets knew.

The Chanter's House,
Ottery St Mary,
Devon

PREFACE AND ACKNOWLEDGEMENTS

In writing, however briefly, about the West Country years of Coleridge and Wordsworth, I have been constantly aware of many debts to those who have written before me. Mrs Henry Sandford in 1888 provided the first and still indispensable book on the subject with her biography of Tom Poole, Coleridge's Nether Stowey friend; Berta Lawrence, drawing on wide knowledge of Quantock history, presented much new information in her book *Coleridge and Wordsworth in Somerset*, published in 1970; and more recent studies by Molly Lefebure, Richard Holmes, Stephen Gill and Nicholas Roe have all added considerably to our understanding of both poets during the period they spent together in the West Country.

This book arose from the belief that there remained, nevertheless, something more to be said, and especially that the West Country itself had seldom been presented in sufficiently accurate detail for its importance in the lives of Coleridge and Wordsworth to be properly understood. For Coleridge, in particular, his experience of the West Country from childhood until early adult life was central to the person he became, and no account of him is complete which fails to emphasize the 'fields & woods & mountains' which, he told his brother George in March 1798, he loved with 'almost a visionary fondness'.[1] In words and pictures, this book attempts the modest but necessary task of redressing a balance, giving prominence to the settings in which extraordinary creative achievements were brought to fulfilment. At the same time, it retells what must always remain one of the most remarkable stories in the history of English literature.

I have been helped by many people in the course of writing the book and gathering illustrations for it. At Ottery St Mary, Lord Coleridge not only allowed me to see the genealogical papers of the late Alwyne Coleridge, but generously agreed to provide a foreword; Ottery's historian, John Whitham, told me about the town, as did Lord Iddesleigh at Upton Pyne. At Nether Stowey I have to thank Rosemary Cawthray, the former custodian of Coleridge Cottage, and her successor Derek Wolff, as well as Reggie Watters of the Coleridge Bookshop, Mr and Mrs John Stacey, Sheelagh Lang, and Carolyn Hilliard. John and Elspeth Scothern showed me Alfoxden; Ian Brereton provided much information on the house and his St Albyn ancestors; and David Payne clarified for me the geography of the Alfoxden area. Lady Elton and Derek and Jane Lilley gave help at Clevedon, as did Francis Greenacre, Sheena Stoddard, and Karin Walton at the City Museum and Art Gallery in Bristol. For help with illustrations I am particularly grateful to the Somerset Archaeological and Natural History Society, Alan and Doreen Marsh, Alan R. Taylor, Kit Houghton, Paula Lewis, Lady Gass, Dr Katherine Wyndham, Anthony Pretor-Pinney, Russell Gore-Andrews, Lawrence Dopson, and Mr and Mrs Tony Richards, as well as to Richard Sainsbury and QPC Photography. Quotations from the collected letters of Samuel Taylor Coleridge and of William and Dorothy Wordsworth are made by permission of Oxford University Press.

I owe much to the helpfulness of friends and colleagues. Alistair Jolly shared his wide knowledge of the Romantic poets, and John Wilkins and Heather Chadwick gave encouragement at Exeter, as did Sarah Lewin at Winchester. At the Somerset Record Office, Adam Green and Liz Park were more helpful than I had a right to expect; Peter Collings willingly solved many photographic problems; Jim Skeggs and Mervyn Richens told me about natural history; and my other colleagues patiently answered numerous questions about West Somerset. Dr Robert Dunning and Mary Siraut allowed me to see unpublished work for the *Victoria County History* and David Bromwich introduced me to the riches at Taunton Castle. To John Dallimore I owe particular thanks for having established the architectural history of Coleridge Cottage for the first time.

Finally, I must thank Roger Thorp at Alan Sutton Publishing for his expertise and his patience, and my family who have throughout given their help and encouragement.

Stoke St Mary,
Somerset.
August, 1991

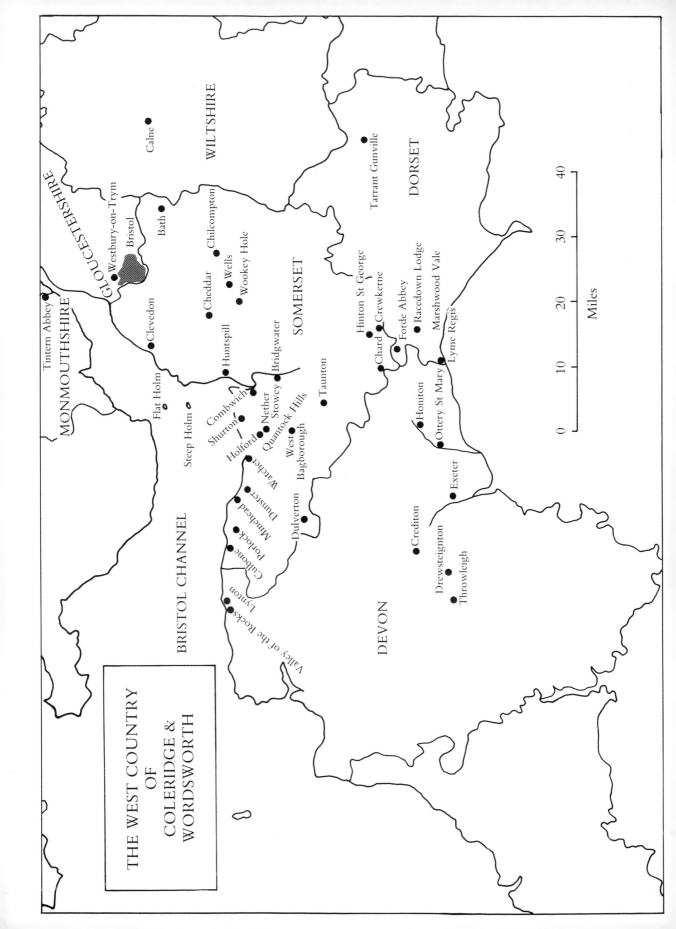

THE WEST COUNTRY
OF
COLERIDGE &
WORDSWORTH

MONMOUTHSHIRE

GLOUCESTERSHIRE

WILTSHIRE

Tintern Abbey ●

Westbury-on-Trym ●
Bristol
Bath ●
Calne ●

Clevedon ●
Cheddar ●
Chilcompton ●
Wells ●
Wookey Hole ●

Flat Holm ●
Huntspill ●

SOMERSET

DORSET

Tarrant Gunville ●

Hinton St George ●
Crewkerne ●
Chard ●
Forde Abbey ●
Racedown Lodge ●
Marshwood Vale

Steep Holm

Combwich ●
Shurton ●
Holford ●
Nether Stowey ●
Bridgwater ●
West Bagborough ●
Quantock Hills
Taunton ●

Watchet
Minehead ●
Dunster ●
Porlock ●
Culbone ●
Dulverton ●

BRISTOL CHANNEL

Lynton ●
Valley of the Rocks

Lyme Regis ●
Honiton ●
Ottery St Mary ●

Exeter ●
Crediton ●

DEVON

Drewsteignton ●
Throwleigh ●

Miles
40
30
20
10
0

Introduction

Early on a summer morning near the end of May 1796, Samuel Taylor Coleridge, thoughtful and preoccupied, was alone in the Somerset town of Bridgwater. He had arrived there following a brief visit to his Somerset friend, Tom Poole of Nether Stowey. But the carrier's van to take him onward to his home in Bristol did not leave until nine o'clock, and with no better means of subduing 'anxious thoughts', he wandered the banks of the muddy River Parrett – 'as filthy as if all the Parrots in the House of Commons had been washing their Consciences therein' – and crossed the market-place to inspect the hustings newly erected for the forthcoming elections: 'I mounted it & pacing the boards mused on Bribery, False Swearing, and other *foibles* of Election Times.'[1]

Coleridge had good reason to be preoccupied. Married for less than a year, and now soon to be a father, he was confronted for almost the first time in his life with the urgent need to earn a living, and looked back, in the years just gone, on humiliations and bitter disappointments. His fitfully brilliant university career had ended without a degree in 1794, partly in consequence of his half-mad decision to enlist in the dragoons; his plans to establish an ideal community in America with Robert Southey had foundered on the hard rocks of practicality and temperamental differences; and only two weeks before his morning walk through the streets of Bridgwater, Coleridge's periodical, the *Watchman*, the result of prodigious and almost single-handed labours, had appeared for the tenth and final time, leaving substantial debts behind it. 'I must do something', he wrote desperately to Tom Poole in July. '. . . Those two Giants, yclept BREAD & CHEESE, bend me into compliance.'[2]

Though his immediate financial crisis was solved, as so often, by his friends, Coleridge at the age of twenty-three seemed trapped by past failure and present indecision, and knew that the choices which the following months would force upon him might shape the whole of his future life. He tried hard to be practical, and considered becoming a journalist, or a schoolmaster, or even a Unitarian minister. Instead, on the last day of 1796, he retraced the route from Bristol to Nether Stowey and settled in a tiny cottage in Stowey's poorest street. His decision owed little either to practicality or to worldly prudence; but his instinct was sound, and in the eighteen months that followed, he found a greater degree of creative fulfilment than he would ever know again.

Bridgwater in the late eighteenth century. Lithograph after a drawing by John Chubb, later a friend of Coleridge'

In choosing to live at Nether Stowey, Coleridge was in important ways returning home. He had been born the son of a Devonshire clergyman in 1772, and the distinctive patterns of the West Country landscape had been familiar to him since childhood. Broad vales, 'rich and elmy fields',[3] and high solitary hills helped to form his earliest conceptions of natural beauty, and his discovery of West Somerset was the discovery of a place already half understood.

He found not only natural beauty in Somerset, but also formative and enduring friendship, first with the steady, dependable Tom Poole, the Stowey tanner, then with William and Dorothy Wordsworth, who, in July 1797, were persuaded by Coleridge to take a year's tenancy of Alfoxden, a mansion which fortuitously stood empty only three miles from Nether Stowey.[4] Their arrival completed that brief, unforeseeable conjunction of personalities in a landscape which was to give rise, in the months that followed, to poetry which has remained among the most familiar in the language, and in which hindsight has identified the beginning of English Romanticism.

The '*Annus Mirabilis*' which produced 'Kubla Khan', 'The Rime of the Ancient Mariner', and 'Tintern Abbey' ended promptly at midsummer 1798 when the tenancy of Alfoxden was given up. Two years later, Coleridge and Wordsworth settled close to one another in the Lake District; but the subtle equilibrium of their relationship had been disturbed, and Coleridge's increasing addiction to opium drew him into a dark world of creative paralysis and physical suffering from which he would never fully re-emerge. Soon, for both men, their memories of the West Country called up what seemed a brief golden age of friendship and creativity, a time of marvels which could never be recaptured.

As he waited in Bridgwater that summer morning in 1796, Coleridge was far from realizing how Nether Stowey and Alfoxden, Tom Poole and the Words-worths, were to be significant in his future life. Present anxiety filled his mind, and the large breakfast he ordered at the inn was eaten, he said, 'purely for the purpose of amusing myself'. Having finished breakfast, he wrote a hasty but heartfelt note to Tom Poole, and shortly afterwards was safely inside the carrier's van as it rattled out of the town and travelled north on the turnpike road to Bristol.

Chapter One

'VISIONS OF CHILDHOOD'

The market town of Ottery St Mary lies in a broad Devon valley eleven miles from the city of Exeter. The River Otter, Coleridge's 'dear native brook', borders the town to the west, and makes its leisurely way through a landscape which to eighteenth-century inhabitants seemed 'the richest finest Country in the world', and which even now preserves the striking beauty which so impressed itself on Coleridge's young mind. The little manor-house at Cadhay stands near at hand in the Ottery meadows, and more distant views reach as far as the great hill-fort at Hembury, built on a commanding spur of land in the late Iron Age. The town itself is in most respects unremarkable by comparison with its Devon neighbours, and like many of them flourished especially in the seventeenth century, heyday of the West Country cloth trade: when Celia Fiennes passed close by in 1698, she found all Exeter and the country around making 'an incredible quantity of serges' which were sent from the port of Topsham to be sold in Europe.[1]

Only at the top of Silver Street, beyond an area in which Ottery's weekly market was anciently held, does the town reveal its more distinctive self. There on a ridge of high ground overlooking Ottery's narrow streets rises the great collegiate church of St Mary, a version, on a smaller scale, of the cathedral church in Exeter. The history of St Mary's and that of the town over which it presides have been bound together since the Middle Ages, and the church's sober, dignified presence was to form part of Coleridge's earliest recollections of childhood. Long and low, with transept towers and a vaulted nave, the building as it stands today was largely the work of Bishop Grandison of Exeter, a 'magnificent and diligent prelate' who ruled over the diocese in the fourteenth century. He chose Ottery as the place in which to found a religious community, and in 1337 obtained the king's licence to make the church a collegiate foundation, whose members were to include a warden, a minister, a chanter, and eight choral vicars. Houses to accommodate them rose as a compact group south of the churchyard, and the church itself was soon ambitiously transformed to provide the setting for an elaborate cycle of daily worship.[2]

Though the Reformation brought an end to Grandison's college, the medieval college houses were allowed to remain, and the collegiate church, to which a magnificent parish aisle had recently been added, was given over completely to

The collegiate church
of St Mary, Ottery
St Mary, in the late
nineteenth century

the people of the town. The medieval choir school also survived – though
renamed by Henry VIII 'the Kynges Newe Grammer Scole of Seynt Marie
Oterey' – and like many provincial grammar schools throughout the land it
continued to provide a modest education of the kind which gave to the youthful
Shakespeare his 'small Latin, and less Greek'.[3]

It was of this school, the King's School, that the Revd John Coleridge became
master on 20 August 1760, four months before also being appointed vicar of the
parish church. He settled with his growing family in the schoolmaster's house,
close to the sixteenth-century schoolroom, and there, on an October morning in
1772, his second wife, Ann Coleridge, gave birth to their tenth and final child. As
with so many details in the life of Samuel Taylor Coleridge, the exact date of his
birth has not gone undisputed. Coleridge himself long believed that he was born
on 20 October, but his father, with a clergyman's attention to such matters,

5

The schoolmaster's house, Ottery St Mary, shortly befo its demolition in 1884. Coleridge wa born in the house c 21 October 1772

recorded in the parish register that the true date was 21 October 'about eleven o'clock in the forenoon'. John Coleridge was then fifty-three years old, his wife forty-five. Their son was brought for baptism in the parish church on 30 December, his godfather, a local man called Samuel Taylor, providing the child with two distinctive names. Thus was young Sam (as his family, to his later great distaste, was apt to call him) or STC (as he preferred to call himself) given his earliest identity in the eyes of the world.[4]

☆

View from the churchyard at Throwleigh, Devon, the parish in which Coleridge's grandfather was born

The family of which Coleridge became a member would have seemed exceptional even had he never been born. His father had risen to a leading position in the town of Ottery from a background of extreme poverty, and Coleridge's surviving brothers were all gifted men whose descendants were to include not only scholars and bishops, but the Lord Chief Justice of England. Social status, so quickly achieved, made the family unwilling in later years to acknowledge their very humble origins. Only Coleridge could see no reason to obscure the truth, and would quote *Macbeth* to the effect that their grandfather, another John, had been 'ditch-delivered by a drab'. Carrying through life a heavy sense that early separation from Ottery had left him no better than an orphan, Coleridge took comfort in believing that his own grandfather had been an orphan before him, a nameless, parentless child, discovered beneath a Devon sky. The truth itself was only slightly more prosaic.[5]

John Coleridge was probably the bastard child of that name baptised on 18 April 1686 at Throwleigh, a remote and beautiful parish on the eastern edge of Dartmoor. His mother was Jane Coleridge, a native of the neighbouring parish of Drewsteignton, and his father, as Coleridge later claimed, was probably William Northmore (1640–1716), member of a substantial Devon family and owner of Wonson Manor in Throwleigh. Northmore's bastard son was destined to gain nothing from his relationship to a wealthy family. 'Christened, educated, & apprenticed by the parish', he married at Drewsteignton in 1715, then migrated to Crediton, where he ultimately became a 'respectable Woolen-draper'. His eldest surviving son, Coleridge's father, was born in 1719 and attended the Grammar School at Crediton; but when bankruptcy brought the family low, the younger John, not quite sixteen years of age, 'walked off to seek his fortune', taking with him no more than his father's blessing and half a crown.[6]

He became a successful schoolmaster, through the kindly help of a family friend, and was a married man with three daughters by the time he walked to Cambridge in 1748 to become an undergraduate at Sidney Sussex College. There he 'distinguished himself for Hebrew & Mathematics', and might eventually have obtained a fellowship had he still been single. Instead, in 1749, he came home to Devon to take charge of Squire's Endowed Latin School in South Molton, and at the end of the year was ordained by the Bishop of Exeter. When his first wife died in 1751, he went so far as to obtain a licence to marry a certain Hannah Laskey. But that wedding evidently did not take place, and in December 1753 it was Ann Bowden whom he rushed to the altar in Exeter, his bride being already heavily pregnant with the first of their many offspring.[7]

The new Mrs Coleridge was born in Bishop's Nympton in 1727 and came from a family whose origins were in the Exmoor borderlands of Devon and Somerset. Strong-willed and ambitious for her children, she did not retain the affection of her youngest child, Samuel, despite her early devotion to him, and left him in adult life with an obscure and painful sense that she had treated him cruelly. Coleridge associated far happier memories with his father, a learned, generous, and notoriously absent-minded man who 'in . . . excessive ignorance of the world' reminded his devoted son of Fielding's Parson Adams. John Coleridge would startle his Sunday congregations by quoting Hebrew to them in his sermons – Hebrew being, as he explained, the 'immediate language of the Holy Ghost' – and published a Latin grammar in which he proposed the 'bold Innovation' of renaming the ablative case the quippe-quare-quale-quia-quidditive case. 'My Father made the world his confidant with respect to his Learning & ingenuity,' Coleridge wrote, '& the world seems to have kept the secret very faithfully.'[8]

Of the nine sons and one daughter born to this remarkable and ill-assorted

The Revd John
Coleridge (1719–81)
with his horse,
outside one of the
former collegiate
buildings at Ottery
St Mary. After a
watercolour of
c. 1775

couple, only the second son failed to survive childhood. Of the rest, some were
already leaving Ottery to begin their careers by the time Coleridge's own
memories began, and he grew up in the schoolmaster's house chiefly among the
younger family members who remained. Next in age to him was his brother
Frank, born in 1770; then followed his sister Ann (or Nancy), dearly loved and
lost early, then his brothers Luke and George. George, who was eight years old

when Coleridge was born, became almost a second father to him in the difficult years ahead, and was, Coleridge wrote, 'every way nearer to Perfection than any man I ever yet knew – indeed, he is worth the whole family in a Lump.'[9]

Coleridge's recollections of his Ottery childhood survive chiefly in the resonant and deeply-felt autobiographical letters which he wrote at Tom Poole's request during 1797–8. As he recorded in the letters, he carried from his earliest years one overriding impression, which was quickly summarized: 'My Father was very fond of me, and I was my mother's darling – in consequence, I was very miserable.' His brother Frank hated him because of their mother's devotion to the new favourite, and Frank's 'immoderately fond' nurse was equally resentful, giving Coleridge 'only thumps & ill names'. So powerful a mixture of love and rejection was both perplexing and formative, leaving the child uncertain where to attach his affections, and desperate in his search for acceptance and approval. '. . . I became fretful, & timorous, & a tell-tale – & the School-boys drove me from play, & were always tormenting me – & hence I took no pleasure in boyish sports.' While Frank was 'climbing, fighting, playing, & robbing orchards', Coleridge was more likely to be found in the meadows by the River Otter – first of those rivers, brooks and springs that were to work so powerfully on his mind – or close by at the sandstone cavern known as Pixies' Parlour, where with the

Pixies' Parlour, a sandstone cavern one mile south of Ottery St Mary. In the summer of 1793 Coleridge visited the cavern with a party of young ladies, 'one of whom, of stature elegantly small, and of complexion colourless yet clear, was proclaimed the Faery Queen'

'hand of . . . childhood' he carved his initials in the rock. As he later recorded in his 'Lines on an Autumnal Evening', these were the settings in which for the first time 'young Poesy/Stared wildly-eager in her noontide dream'.[10]

He read voraciously, developing his early appetite for books on visits to the shop in Crediton kept by his Aunt Susannah. There the young Coleridge would read anything he could find, and at the age of six had already progressed from the tales of Tom Hickathrift and Jack the Giant-Killer to *Robinson Crusoe* and *The Arabian Nights*. The story of a man compelled to search for a pure virgin, read one evening while his mother was mending stockings, left him 'haunted by spectres' whenever he was in the dark; other stories drew him out to the churchyard, where, with his imagination overflowing, he would race up and down through the great avenue of elm trees, and act out among the docks, nettles and rank grass whatever he had been reading. From his knowledge of 'Romances, & Relations of Giants & Magicians, & Genii', his mind was soon 'habituated *to the Vast*'; and when, walking home to Ottery one winter evening, his father told him the names of the stars 'and how Jupiter was a thousand times larger than our world – and

The King's Grammar School, Ottery St Mary, shortly before its demolition in 1884

11

Sir Stafford
Northcote (1762–
1851), 7th baronet.
He succeeded to the
baronetcy in 1770,
and was not yet
twenty years old
when he rescued
Coleridge from
probable death on
the banks of the
River Otter. Portrait
by James Northcote,
RA

that the other twinkling stars were Suns that had worlds rolling round them',
Coleridge listened with profound delight, 'but without the least mixture of
wonder or incredulity'.[11]

His first formal education was received in the reading school kept at Ottery by
'Old Dame Key', a relative of Sir Joshua Reynolds, and at six years old he
progressed to his father's grammar school, where he quickly surpassed all his
contemporaries. The old women of the town marvelled at a child whose intellect
had been 'forced into almost an unnatural ripeness', and their flattery made him
vain:

I . . . despised most of the boys, that were at all near my own age – and before I
was eight years old, I was a *character* – sensibility, imagination, vanity, sloth, &
feelings of deep & bitter contempt for almost all who traversed the orbit of my
understanding, were even then prominent & manifest.[12]

His emotional vulnerability was no less manifest, and in early quarrels was easily exploited. One argument with Frank, who soon grew 'very fond' of his unfathomable young brother, led to a childhood crisis whose significance Coleridge was still struggling to understand far into adult life. 'I had asked my mother one evening to cut my cheese *entire*, so that I might toast it,' he told Tom Poole:

> This was no easy matter, it being a *crumbly* cheese – My mother however did it – I went into the garden for something or other, and in the mean time my Brother Frank *minced* my cheese, 'to disappoint the favorite'.[13]

In the violent argument which followed, Coleridge was prevented from running at his brother with a knife by the return of their mother, and then fled from the house, still in an 'agony of passion', stopping only when he reached a hill overlooking the River Otter a mile from the town. He obstinately remained there even when his anger had subsided, and read morning and evening prayers from a little shilling book he had with him, thinking at the same time 'with inward & gloomy satisfaction' how miserable his mother must be. He saw Mr Vaughan cross Cadhay Bridge a few hundred yards away, heard the calves in fields beyond the river calling to their mothers, and then, as the storms of an October night closed round, he closed his eyes and tried to sleep.

Mrs Coleridge was quite as distracted by her son's disappearance as he could have wished. Men and boys were sent to look for him, the ponds and the river were dragged, and by morning hopes of finding him alive had almost been given up. Coleridge had rolled in his sleep down the hill slope to within a few yards of the river, and when he woke up at dawn, he found he was unable to move or even to call out to the shepherds and workmen he could see near by. Only the perseverance of Sir Stafford Northcote, who lived at the Warden's House, managed to save him. Sir Stafford had been searching all night, and finally came so close that he heard the child crying:

> He carried me in his arms, for near a quarter of a mile; when we met my father & Sir Stafford's servants. – I remember, & never shall forget, my father's face as he looked upon me while I lay in the servant's arms – so calm, and the tears stealing down his face: for I was the child of his old age.

His mother was 'outrageous with joy' at the return of her lost child, and put him to bed, where in a day or two he recovered. But the after-effects of his experience remained with him far longer. He was subject to attacks of ague for many years, and memories of that October night came to embody for him his sense of exile from his family, and his anger at his mother's demanding and erratic love.[14]

☆

Towards the end of September 1781, John Coleridge took his son Frank to Plymouth, where he was to begin service as a midshipman under Admiral Graves of Cadhay. Returning to Ottery late on 4 October, Mr Coleridge gave a 'long & particular account' of his journey, before going to bed in high spirits. Soon afterwards, his wife heard a noise in his throat, and when she spoke to him, he did not reply. Her shriek awakened the house, and Coleridge, who had been asleep when his father returned, knew at once what it signified, saying to himself in the darkness, 'Papa is dead.'[15]

John Coleridge, 'an Israelite without guile', had probably died of a massive stoke, and a few days later was buried on the north side of the altar in the church he had served for twenty-one years. The practical effects of his death on a largely unprovided family were immediate, and soon after the funeral Mrs Coleridge and her children moved from the schoolhouse to make way for her husband's successor as schoolmaster. A more dramatic change for the youngest family member came in the new year. Though Coleridge continued at the King's School for several months, delighting his mother by pointing out the new master's faulty knowledge of grammar, in April 1782 Francis Buller, a family friend and later an eminent judge, obtained for him a presentation to Christ's Hospital in London (the Blue Coat School), 'there to be educated, and brought up among other poor children'. Mrs Coleridge may have felt that the Blue Coat School would best prepare her son for the clerical career John Coleridge had wished him to follow. To Coleridge himself, however, his enforced departure from Ottery seemed like betrayal. At the age of only nine, he set off on the London coach, and said a sudden and bewildered farewell both to his family and to his Devon childhood.[16]

Exile from the West Country was to last far longer than Coleridge can have expected. His first surviving letter, written to his mother in February 1785, seems to suggest that he had visited Ottery in the recent past; but better evidence that he returned there does not survive until 1789, seven years after his arrival in London. By that time his feelings of resentment against his mother were fixed for life, and the imaginative intensity with which he called up the Devon landscape as a lost Eden of content had become a habit of mind. Coleridge was to speak and write on many occasions of the 'visions of childhood' which so filled him during his London school-days. He told Wordsworth how he would lie on the leads, or flat roof, of Christ's Hospital, and gaze into the sky because that was the only face of nature London could not obscure, or how he would close his eyes and 'by internal light' see before him the trees and meadows of Ottery and the river itself.[17] In important respects, however, his longing was a self-deception, a poetically fruitful means of expressing that sense of loneliness and isolation which had been as much a part of him in Ottery as in London. Only when he settled as a newly-married man, first at Clevedon, and later at Nether Stowey, was he able to

Cadhay Bridge and the River Otter

14

Left: The cloisters of Christ's Hospital, Newgate Street, London. The school buildings were demolished in 1902. *Right*: The Revd James Boyer (1736–1814), Upper Master of the Grammar School, Christ's Hospital

test the healing powers of mere natural beauty, and to find that beauty was not enough.

Christ's Hospital had been founded in 1553 for the 'orphaned, aged and sick poor', but by the time of Coleridge's arrival it had long outgrown its origins to become the foremost of England's charity schools. Seven hundred boys, almost a third of them sons of the clergy, lived their 'ultra-Spartan' lives in an institution which combined frequently brutal discipline with a consistently meagre diet. 'Every morning a bit of dry bread & some bad small beer,' Coleridge mournfully recalled, 'every evening a larger piece of bread, & cheese or butter . . .' Dinner was an unvarying weekly round in which boiled beef and mutton figured largely, and it was little compensation to several hundred hungry schoolboys that they took their meals in the school's magnificent hall, overlooked by the demure and decorative paintings of Antonio Verrio.[18]

Coleridge, the 'playless day-dreamer',[19] survived and made friends at Christ's Hospital in spite of every misery his school-days could heap on him. His isolated Ottery childhood had provided few opportunities for exploring the possibilities of friendship. Now, adrift from home and more vulnerable than ever, he discovered in himself a remarkable gift for inspiring friendship, a gift which never left him. In the nine years he remained at school his closest companions were to include Bob Allen, Val le Grice, and Thomas Middleton; but no friend proved more lasting or dependable than the gifted, tongue-tied Charles Lamb, son of a minor official at the Inner Temple. For Lamb, the desolation of the exiled Coleridge had a poignant force, which he famously recalled in his essay 'Christ's Hospital Five and Thirty Years Ago'. There, speaking in Coleridge's voice and tactfully substituting Calne for Ottery, he wrote:

> O the cruelty of separating a poor lad from his early homestead! The yearnings which I used to have towards it in those unfledged years! How, in my dreams, would my native town (far in the west) come back, with its church, and trees, and faces! How I would wake weeping, and in the anguish of my heart exclaim upon sweet Calne in Wiltshire![20]

The refuge of books, first discovered in his Aunt Susannah's shop, still remained available to him in London, and by a curious accident he gained access to as many books as even he could want. Walking one day down a London street, arms outstretched as he day-dreamt that he was Leander swimming the Hellespont, he was accused by a man whose coat he touched of being a pick-pocket. Coleridge's improbably romantic explanation and evident intelligence so impressed the man that he gave the remarkable child a subscription to the circulating library in Cheapside, where he began, according to his own not unlikely account, to read every book it contained. 'Conceive what I must have been at fourteen,' he reminisced to James Gillman, his first biographer. '. . . My whole being was, with eyes closed to every object of present sense, to crumple myself up in a sunny corner, and read, read, read.' He was guilty of no more than his usual exaggeration when, at the age of twenty-four, he announced to a friend that he had read 'almost every thing'.[21]

Coleridge's outstanding abilities remained quite unsuspected at Christ's Hospital until they came to the attention of the Upper Grammar School master, the Revd James Boyer, a man whose great gifts as a teacher were only exceeded by his sadistically violent temper. With the mellowing of harsh memories, Coleridge was able in middle age to speak of Boyer's teaching as an 'inestimable advantage', even while admitting that his old master's severity still haunted his dreams. It was Boyer who helped Coleridge to understand the subtle logic and 'fugitive causes' which gave the greatest poetry its power, and who taught the lesson, not immediately applied in Coleridge's teenage work, that conventional metaphors and needless elaboration seldom made good verse:

> In fancy I can almost hear him now, exclaiming 'Harp? Harp? Lyre? Pen and ink, boy, you mean! Muse, boy, Muse? your Nurse's daughter, you mean! Pierian spring? Oh 'aye! the cloister-pump, I suppose!'[22]

At the age of sixteen, Coleridge joined the select band of the 'Grecians', the school's most gifted pupils who studied for places at Oxford and Cambridge. In the three years that followed, he at last found personal happiness and intellectual fulfilment, and was swiftly transformed into the brilliantly eloquent young man the greater world was soon to know. It was that young man, declaiming and arguing, whom Charles Lamb was famously to invoke: 'Come back into memory, like as thou wert in the day-spring of thy fancies,' he wrote in 1820, 'with hope like a fiery column before thee – the dark pillar not yet turned – Samuel Taylor Coleridge – Logician, Metaphysician, Bard!'

> How have I seen the casual passer through the Cloisters stand still, intranced with admiration (while he weighed the disproportion between the *speech* and the *garb* of the young Mirandula), to hear thee unfold, in thy deep and sweet intonations, the mysteries of Jamblichus, or Plotinus (for even in those years thou waxedst not pale at such philosophic draughts), or reciting Homer in his Greek, or Pindar – while the walls of the old Grey Friars re-echoed to the accents of the *inspired charity-boy*![23]

The destruction of the Bastille in July 1789 drew from Coleridge impassioned verse in praise of freedom and 'glad Liberty', and the fevered excitement inspired throughout Europe by the early days of the French Revolution provided the intellectual climate in which his radical conscience began to form. His reading of Voltaire's *Philosophical Dictionary* made him briefly an atheist (Boyer beat religion back into him, to lifelong effect), but of more lasting consequence was his discovery of twenty-one sonnets by a Wiltshire clergyman called William Lisle Bowles (1762–1850). The sonnets of Bowles struck Coleridge with the force of revelation, seeming to him, in their natural use of language and heartfelt expression of personal feeling, unlike anything he had ever read. He made over forty transcriptions of the sonnets 'as the best presents I could offer to those, who had in any way won my regard', and in his own poetic experiments of the next few years found an important model in the work of the now-forgotten Wiltshire priest.[24]

New friendships, as much as politics and poetry, transformed for him the final years of school. He was introduced by Tom Evans, a younger school friend, to his widowed mother Mrs Evans, and was soon being welcomed with unaffected warmth into the family home near Christ's Hospital. He came to love the generous and practical Mrs Evans like the mother he felt he had now entirely lost, and for her daughters developed feelings altogether more romantic. He and Bob Allen enjoyed 'hours of paradise' escorting the Miss Evanses home on Saturdays, and would bring them 'the pillage of the flower-gardens . . . with sonnet or love-rhyme wrapped round the nose-gay'.[25] He became devoted most of all to Mary Evans, the eldest daughter, and believed that he loved her. But by the time he arrived at Jesus College, Cambridge, in 1791, having left Christ's Hospital with academic honour and real regret, his love had not become a sufficiently urgent reality for him to declare it. Instead, it remained a pleasing abstraction, like his fading memories of the Devon fields.

☆

Jesus College,
Cambridge, in 1841

Cambridge was empty when Coleridge reached it in October. The fenland winds blew through a town 'very fertile in alleys, and mud, and cats, and dogs . . .' but almost devoid of the friends who had increasingly sustained him at Christ's Hospital. His old friend and mentor, Thomas Middleton, now in his final year at Pembroke College, was the only person he knew, and it was Middleton who in the months ahead provided Coleridge with fatherly guidance and approval. Though Coleridge was lonely, and made ill by the dampness of his rooms, he quickly became a regular attender at chapel, read mathematics for three hours a day, and in 'Leisure hours' was making translations of Anacreon. Coleridge was the first to recognize that '*Freshmen* always *begin* very *furiously*'; but so long as Middleton was at hand to guide and encourage, he overcame the weakness of will and habit of procrastination which were always ready to disable him. By April 1792, he was 'writing for *all* the prizes', and later that year his 'Ode on the Slave

19

Trade', a poem 'tinged with melancholy & moral pathos', won the Browne Medal.[26]

He spent his first summer from Cambridge in leisurely visits to his family, staying first with his brother Edward in Salisbury then travelling to Ottery for one of the few lengthy returns he had made since childhood.[27] The reality of the narrow market town belied his long-nurtured recollections of it, and some of those he had loved most were now gone. His brother Luke, whom Coleridge had come to know and revere in London, had died in 1790 at the age of twenty-five; Nancy, loved 'most tenderly', had succumbed to tuberculosis the following year at only twenty-one. He amused himself during his visit writing doggerel about the Revd Fullwood Smerdon, his father's successor, and returned to Cambridge reflecting with distaste on Devonshire people:

> The manners of the Inhabitants annihilated whatever tender ideas of pleasure my Fancy rather than my Memory had pictured to my Expectation. I found them (almost universally) to be gross without openness, and cunning without refinement.[28]

This new assessment of his home marked an important casting off, a kind of liberation, and if in later years Ottery remained symbolically important to Coleridge, that was only because his recollections of the shaping years of childhood all seemed to gather at the town. As a present reality, Ottery had ceased to compel him.

In Cambridge that autumn he found himself without the steadying influence of Thomas Middleton, and without money. To his growing band of Cambridge friends he remained the brilliant talker and philosopher whose radical sympathies were ever more plain. Privately, however, his mood was often near despair as he contemplated the financial and emotional chaos into which he was sinking. 'I am so closely blocked up by an army of Misfortunes,' he told Mary Evans in one of his increasingly fond letters, 'that really there is no passage left open for Mirth or any thing else.' When he visited Ottery in August 1793 his brothers reluctantly agreed to help him; but some of the money they supplied was frittered away on the journey back to Cambridge, and when he got there he discovered a host of forgotten debts. 'My Agitations were delirium,' he later told George:

> I formed a Party, dashed to London at eleven o'clock at night, and for three days lived in all the tempest of Pleasure . . . I again returned to Cambridge – staid a week – such a week! Where Vice has not annihilated Sensibility, there is little need of a Hell![29]

By late November, in a mood not far from suicidal, he was in London once more, desperately hoping for a win in the Irish Lottery; but when that last hope failed, he used the only means he could find of acting decisively. On 2 December

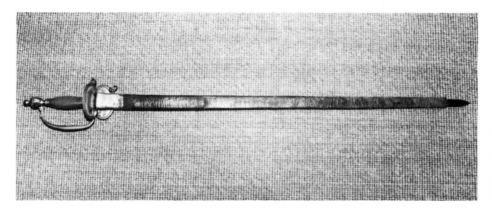

Sword used by Coleridge as a recruit in the 15th Light Dragoons. It is now preserved at his cottage in Nether Stowey

1793, having adopted the alias of Silas Tomkyn Comberbache, he secretly enlisted in the 15th Light Dragoons.[30]

☆

Like the child who long before had fled from the schoolmaster's house at Ottery, Coleridge in his flight to the dragoons was escaping from intolerable external pressures, from the certain disapproval of his family, and from emotions within himself he seemed unable to control. His descent into drunkenness and sexual dissipation filled him with self-disgust, and his still undeclared love for Mary Evans was gaining a disturbing power. Now, dressed as a soldier, and further hidden behind his remarkable new name, he closed his eyes on his troubles and tried to forget.

He was posted first to Reading, and was soon proving himself a soldier and horseman of rare incompetence. He gained the trust and friendship of his comrades by writing their love-letters, and for a month in the pest-house at Henley became the devotedly unselfish nurse of a soldier suffering from smallpox. It was there that a letter from his brother George eventually reached him, forwarded by one of Coleridge's friends who had discovered the full story of his flight from Cambridge. George was generous and conciliatory to an extent that Coleridge can hardly have expected. But the joint efforts of George and James Coleridge to rescue their brother from his folly were to prove both complex and time-consuming. At first the army would not consider a discharge before a substitute had been supplied. Eventually, submitting to James Coleridge's persuasion and recognizing the peculiar circumstances, the authorities decided on another solution, though one of which the Coleridge family evidently remained unaware. On 10 April 1794, Silas Tomkyn Comberbache was discharged from the dragoons, 'being Insane'.[31]

That was a judgement with which the remorseful S.T. Coleridge would, for the moment, hardly have disagreed. 'I laugh almost like an insane person when I cast my eye backward on the prospect of my past two years,' he had written to

Coleridge's brothe James (1759–1836) *left*, and George (1764–1828), *right*. Coleridge thought George 'every wa nearer to Perfectio than any man I ev yet knew'

George in February. 'What a gloomy *Huddle* of eccentric Actions, and dim-discovered motives!' When he returned to college immediately following his discharge, he was lucky to escape with relatively minor punishment – the Master ordered one month's gating and ninety pages of Greek translation – and was determined not only to drop his more unsuitable friends but, as in his first year at Cambridge, 'to write for all the Prizes'.[32] Throughout his life Coleridge found such resolutions far easier to make than to abide by, and in reality his university career was almost at an end, as was any possibility of academic distinction. Remorse, dissatisfaction and hope filled his mind as the heat of a glorious midsummer approached, and his yearning for a means to channel his abundant intellectual and emotional energy was greater now than it had ever been.

In early June, poised between elation and despair, he set out on a walking tour with an amiably dull university friend, Joseph Hucks. By the time Coleridge returned to Jesus College three months later, having travelled to Oxford and Bristol, and tramped half over Wales and Somerset, the landscape of his life, and his hopes for the future, had been dramatically transformed.

Chapter Two

'EPIDEMIC DELUSION'

Coleridge left Cambridge on his summer walking tour with simple intentions. He and Joseph Hucks were to spend 'three or four days' in Oxford, and then to embark on a lengthy exploration of North Wales, the destination at that period of many travellers searching for the picturesque beauty praised by writers such as William Gilpin. For some who made the journey into Wales, the experience was profound: on a warm summer night in 1791 William Wordsworth had climbed to the top of Snowdon to watch the sun rise, and had found there an intensity of natural beauty which he never forgot. Coleridge's Welsh visit, by contrast, was perhaps the least significant part of his wanderings during the next few weeks, and almost from the moment he left Cambridge, his simple plans for what he called his 'peregrination' began to grow more complex.[1]

He reached Oxford with Joseph Hucks about the middle of June 1794, and quickly renewed his friendship with Bob Allen, an undergraduate at University College since leaving Christ's Hospital two years earlier. Allen, in turn, took Coleridge to Balliol to introduce him to a young radical and poet called Robert Southey, who was then almost twenty years old. The two men were instantly captivated by one another, Coleridge overwhelming Southey with his extra-ordinary powers of eloquence and intellect, Southey immediately winning Coleridge's admiration by his decisiveness and strength of character. The pattern of their relationship was to be repeated in many of the 'chance-started friendships' which Coleridge formed in later years. Struggling throughout his life with his own infirmity of will, and with a haunting sense that he was like some great tree possessing *pith within* the Trunk, not heart of Wood', he was consistently drawn, for good and ill, to those possessing stronger personalities than his own.[2]

Southey had been born in 1774 above the draper's shop in Wine Street, Bristol, belonging to his unsuccessful father. His childhood had largely been spent, however, in the more socially elevated household of his snobbish and unloved aunt, Elizabeth Tyler, from whom he may have learnt the polished superficiality of manner which was one feature of his character. When he arrived at Balliol College in 1792, he had recently been expelled from Westminster School for publishing an essay condemning flogging, and his radical temperament developed rapidly during his Oxford years. He supported the French Revolution even more enthusiastically than Coleridge, and in 1793 bitterly opposed the

23

Oxford from the
river, *c.* 1850

willingness of Pitt's government to go to war against the recently proclaimed French Republic. He read Plato, and despairing of his own country, dreamt of an island 'peopled by men who should be Christians and Philosophers and where Vice only should be contemptible'.[3]

Coleridge was not only a willing listener to Southey's ideas, but was soon developing them into grand and Utopian principles during long hours spent in Oxford 'disputing on metaphysical subjects'. The philosophies of Rousseau and of David Hartley, whose work had become a powerful influence on Coleridge, convinced them both that 'Vice is not natural to Man', and that given strong reasons for being virtuous, 'Man would approach very near perfection'.[4] Before

Left: Robert Southey (1774–1843). After a portrait by John Opie, 1804. *Right*: Samuel Taylor Coleridge (1772–1834). After a pencil and chalk drawing by Robert Hancock, 1796

Coleridge's lengthening visit had come to an end, the two dissatisfied young men had pursued the logic of their arguments to a startling conclusion. They decided, with a wild mixture of folly and idealism, that in the spring of 1795 they would set sail from England to establish an ideal community in America, and in the meantime would gather recruits for the scheme and earn money for it by writing.

The community was to be governed according to the principle of 'Pantisocracy' – a word invented by Coleridge meaning 'equal rule by all' – and in the course of the next few months Pantisocracy in its broad details was discussed and argued into existence. The proposed community, to be established on the banks of the Susquehannah river in New England, would consist of twelve men and women, and would sustain itself by farming the land. Coleridge and Southey optimistically calculated that two or three hours daily labour would be all that was required, and that the remaining time could be given up to 'study, liberal discussions, and the education of their children'. Members of the community were to be permitted their own opinions in matters of politics and religion, but property would be held in common.[5]

The astonishing speed with which the two brother radicals developed their Pantisocratic scheme was testimony not only to the transforming effect they had on one another, but to the very weak foundations upon which the whole

Gloucester seen fr
Robins Wood Hil
1829

enterprise rested. Although other idealistic communities were already being established in America at that period, few who saw the Pantisocratic scheme in its early growth were ever convinced that it could succeed. Coleridge and Southey themselves soon became impervious to all doubt. With the certainty of the newly converted, they could see only that Pantisocracy offered an escape from their increasingly unsatisfactory and unhappy lives, and from a country whose politics they deplored. It seemed to promise a new beginning, almost a new birth.

Coleridge had spent three weeks in Oxford before, on 5 July 1794, he finally set off on his Welsh expedition, promising Southey that he would rejoin him later to make further plans for settling in America. Joseph Hucks now seemed a poor companion in comparison with Coleridge's new Oxford friend, and as the two men walked on under a blazing sun, first to Gloucester – 'a nothing-to-be-said-about Town' – and then to Ross-on-Wye, Coleridge's thoughts returned constantly to the substance of his conversations with Southey. 'I have positively done nothing but dream of the System of no Property every step of the Way since I left you,' he wrote back to Oxford on 13 July.[6]

He not only dreamed Pantisocracy, he preached it as well. At Llanvillin his oratory caused two huge butcher-like men to dance about the room in excited admiration, and at Bala, he provoked a violent quarrel among the justice, the doctor, and others of the parish who were gathered at the inn. His invincible capacity for making friends soon prevailed, however, and, as he explained to Southey, 'they all except the Parson shook me by the hand, and said I was an open hearted honest-speaking Fellow, tho' I was a bit of a Democrat'. Only at Wrexham were painful thoughts quite unexpectedly revived: Coleridge caught sight of Mary Evans, and discovered that she was in the town visiting her grandmother. But that sudden reminder of '"thoughts full of bitterness" and images too dearly loved', as he expressed himself theatrically to Southey, subdued his high spirits only briefly. 'Love is a local Anguish,' he wrote after he and Hucks had travelled on from Wrexham. 'I am 50 miles distant, and am not half so miserable.'[7]

On about 5 August, after climbing Penmaenmawr and Snowdon, and experiencing sundry other adventures, Coleridge arrived at the Bush Inn, Bristol, and immediately sought out Robert Southey. Southey had reached the city shortly before, having walked from Oxford with George Burnett, a Balliol friend who had been persuaded to join the Pantisocrats. To his friends in his native city, Southey began with missionary enthusiasm to explain the principles of Pantisocracy and to praise the genius of the absent Coleridge. Southey's seafaring brother, Tom, was an early recruit to the scheme, as was Southey's widowed mother in Bath (even though she told him she thought he was mad). Robert Lovell, a recent Bristol friend of democratic principles, was not so easily persuaded, but before long 'totally changed his opinion' and became an important convert. Lovell was a Bristol poet of minor talents whose rich Quaker family had disowned him for his marriage that year to a beautiful actress called Mary Fricker, one of five sisters already well known to Southey. Indeed, the third sister, the 'mild and affectionate' Edith Fricker, was even now the object of his somewhat calculating attentions, and within a fortnight had accepted his proposal of marriage, together with its Pantisocratic consequences.[8]

It was at Lovell's dinner-table that Coleridge eventually found Southey, and there for the first time that he met Lovell's wife Mary and her eldest sister Sarah Fricker. The eldest Miss Fricker never forgot the arrival of the travel-weary student whose brilliant reputation had gone so powerfully before him. 'Brown as a berry', his clothes worn out, and his hair in need of cutting, he appeared before them as a 'dreadful figure', though one whose torrential eloquence was unabated. Lovell gave Coleridge food that night, but not shelter, and in the days that followed was responsible with Southey for introducing him to a city strong in religious dissent and political radicalism. One meeting of particular significance was with a young dissenting bookseller called Joseph Cottle, whose shop stood at the corner of Corn Street and High Street, a few yards from Southey's birthplace. Cottle, who four years later was to publish the *Lyrical Ballads* and in old age produced his garrulous and unreliable *Reminiscences*, immediately saw in Coleridge the signs of 'commanding genius', but reserved for Southey's 'great suavity of manners' his more enthusiastic praise. Pantisocracy, the everlasting theme, he

At the heart of
Bristol, looking
from Wine Street
into Corn Street,
1829. The building
on the left with the
curved façade had
formerly been Jose
Cottle's bookshop

Joseph Cottle (1770–
1853), friend and
first publisher of
Coleridge,
Wordsworth and
Southey

considered an 'epidemic delusion' of comic potential, a judgement not inappro-
priate to some of Southey's more absurd pronouncements on the subject that
summer, but less than fair to the deep seriousness with which Coleridge had
begun to form his Pantisocratic ideas of social relations and social justice.[9]

In the second week of August, filled by an idealistic vision of their future lives on
the banks of the Susquehannah, Coleridge and Southey set out from Bristol on a
walking tour into Somerset. To Southey, the county was almost home territory.
Although he had been born in Wine Street, Bristol, his cloth-making ancestors
had come from Wellington, and his grandfather had farmed in the remote
Somerset hamlet of Rich's Holford below the southern slopes of the Quantock
Hills; his eccentric uncle, John, was comfortably established in a 'most delightful
villa' a mile from Taunton, and Bath had intermittently been Southey's own
home since childhood.[10]

   It was to Bath that the two Pantisocrats walked first, staying the night at old
Mrs Southey's house, 8 Westgate Buildings, where another visitor, Sarah
Fricker, was already in residence. Mrs Southey had asked Sarah to visit so they

Wells Cathedral
from the north-ea
1830

could 'talk over the American affair', and it may by then have seemed inevitable to Sarah that she too would be carried on the Pantisocratic tide.[11] Coleridge himself cannot have failed to make the calculation that of four marriageable Fricker sisters, one was married to Robert Lovell, and another all but engaged to Southey. The dangerous logic of events was leading to a predictable conclusion, though Sarah and Coleridge had met for the first time only nine days before and were of fundamentally different temperaments, she sharp-tongued, humorous and practical, he procrastinating and visionary. High hopes and summer weather did nothing to encourage circumspection, and by the time Coleridge and Southey left Bath the next morning, with Southey's dog Rover in attendance, it is likely that some kind of relationship with Sarah was already understood.

The two friends set out on their meandering though scenic way through Somerset intending first to visit George Burnett at his family home in Huntspill. They were ten miles from Bath when they reached the village of Chilcompton, remarkable for a beautiful stream which bordered the village street on one side and which abounded with trout and eels. Coleridge addressed to the stream a delicate poem in the Bowles manner, describing the 'scatter'd cots and peaceful hamlet' he saw, as well as a band of schoolchildren launching their 'paper navies' into the water. It is a poem such as a man would write in contented mood, and

Cheddar Gorge,
looking south, 18

30

Southey for his part thought it 'very beautiful'. They dropped down into the city of Wells from the lower slopes of the Mendip Hills, and cannot have failed to pause for one of the finest views of the cathedral. What else they saw in and near the city they did not record, but it evidently did not include on this occasion the famous caverns at Wookey Hole. Cheddar Gorge, however, was considered indispensable, and towards evening they marched onward.[12]

'How far to Chedder?', they asked everyone they met, receiving estimates which varied from two-and-a-half miles to seven. Night fell, but in spite of that, as Southey wrote to a friend, 'We talked philosophy like two poets and often paused one while to drink at a clear spring – another while to encourage poor Rover now quite lame – and sometimes to mark the glowworms paley ray.' When Cheddar was finally reached at about ten o'clock, no one would take them in, until an innkeeper had pity on them and made up a bed in the garret. Rover insisted on joining them there, the landlady taking care to bolt the door on the outside 'for fear we should rob the house'. Southey did not sleep well: Coleridge, evidently troubled by dreams even when his waking thoughts were optimistic, made a 'vile bedfellow'.[13]

During his Welsh expedition, Coleridge had occasionally lapsed with self-mocking enthusiasm into the prose style of the travel writers to express his feelings for mountains 'sublimely terrible' and other natural marvels. When the sun rose on Cheddar Cliffs – as the gorge was invariably called – he found a scene which justified superlatives, and which travellers had long regarded as among the most remarkable natural sights in lowland Britain. Only Southey's description survives to give some impression of the effect produced by the towering limestone gorge on two minds eager to be astonished:

> Never did I see a grander scene – immense rocks rising perpendicularly from the glen to such a height as pained the neck of the spectator, and terminating in the most bold and fantastic manner. Large trees grew from the interstices of the stone and sheep brouzed on the edge of every precipice.

There was another stream to drink from, perhaps an opportunity to visit some of the gorge's 'five considerable caverns', and in the scene as a whole, images enough for Coleridge to store up for the poetry of the future.[14]

They probably reached George Burnett later that day at Huntspill, where his father's Georgian house stood at a respectable distance from the busy turnpike, with a large sundial presiding over the front door. The elder Burnett can scarcely have been pleased to welcome the two wandering Pantisocrats. He was a prosperous farmer who had sent his son to Balliol – a college which owned land in the parish – with the intention that he should eventually be ordained. Now John Burnett found his good-natured and impressionable son falling under the spell of two far more intelligent men of dubious opinions, and caught up in a wild scheme for emigration to America. Certainly, George Burnett, weak-willed and indolent, was to suffer the most from the rash ideas and too easy friendships which that summer produced. Before he died in 1811, an opium-addicted pauper in Marylebone Workhouse, he may have reflected that it would have been better had he never left the low-lying fields of Huntspill.[15]

Burnett was not the only friend Southey and Coleridge hoped to visit in the course of the Somerset expedition. A few miles from Huntspill, in the hamlet of Shurton, lived Henry Poole, a fellow student of Coleridge's at Jesus College,[16] and one member of a large and talented family whose various branches were scattered through a number of local villages. Coleridge and Southey may have crossed the River Parrett at Bridgwater in order to reach Shurton; more probably, like Thomas De Quincey thirteen years later, they decided to shorten the journey by using the river ferry at Combwich Reach. If so, it was at Combwich (pronounced 'Cummage') that Coleridge first set foot within that secluded, forgotten territory, bounded by the Quantock Hills and a bleakly impressive coastline, which was to remain with him for the rest of his life.

He and Southey found Henry Poole living at his father's house, Shurton Court, then recently transformed from a large farmhouse to a townish Georgian mansion. Henry, who later became the amiable vicar of Cannington, was never a likely recruit to idealistic schemes for emigration. Nor was his father, William Poole, a landowner and practical farmer renowned for his 'astonishing sagacity in

Gravestones of the Burnett family in the churchyard at Huntspill

33

Shurton Court,
Stogursey, the ho
of Henry Poole

predicting the course of the weather'. But the family at Shurton evidently warmed to Coleridge in spite of his views, and it was to Henry's sister Lavinia that he would later address his affectionate short poem 'To a Young Lady on her Recovery from a Fever'.[17] Though Shurton proved to be less than fertile ground for Pantisocracy, Henry Poole was quite happy to guide Coleridge and Southey to more promising territory near at hand. On the morning of Monday 18 August 1794, he accordingly set off with them on the road to Nether Stowey, three miles distant.

Nether Stowey – usually known in Coleridge's day, and since, simply as Stowey – had called itself a town for as long as anyone could remember, but by the late eighteenth century it was in reality no more than a large, straggling village whose inhabitants numbered fewer than six hundred. It lay at the point where the fertile coastal plain to which Shurton belonged gave way to the austerely beautiful Quantock Hills, and in the meeting of those two quite different landscapes the village acquired something of its distinctive character: Stowey was a place always busy with the concerns of a lowland domestic world, but the gateway as well to a solitary hill country where man's dominance was suddenly challenged and nature prevailed. Accidents of history, as much as of geography, had played their part in making the village. The attentions of powerful lords in the Middle Ages brought

The market-house, Nether Stowey, from a watercolour by W.W. Wheatley, 1845. The old woman on the right is walking down Lime Street. On the left is the beginning of Castle Street

borough status, a castle, and the right to hold a market and a fair, and ensured that Stowey was quickly established as one of the most important places between Bridgwater and Williton. Even the decline which came in later centuries was only relative. When Coleridge first entered the village in August 1794, it remained the economic focus of a wide surrounding territory, and struggled, in the midst of endemic rural poverty and untamed nature, to sustain its modest version of prosperous, civilized society.[18]

Approaching from Shurton and Stogursey, Henry Poole and his companions probably entered Stowey from the north. The first they saw of the village may thus have been the dilapidated thatched cottage called Gilberts or Gilbards, which, improbable as it would have seemed to Coleridge in the fever of Pantisocracy, was to have so important a place in his later history.[19] The cottage, the last in the village, stood at the end of Lime Street, one of the three short streets which converged on the centre of the village and at whose junction stood Stowey's ramshackle market-house. Narrow, busy, and densely built, Lime Street was the poorest of the village streets, and probably provided homes for the labourers and artisans – clothworkers, candlemakers, quarrymen and others – who made up a large part of the Stowey community in the late eighteenth century. St Mary's Street, containing three inns and a few grander houses, gave way to open country before reaching St Mary's Church and Stowey Court, the latter a mansion of the sixteenth century with formal gardens and a gazebo. Castle Street, running west from the market-house, formed the broad heart of Stowey, and contained the majority of its more prosperous households. Here lived wealthier tradesmen and professionals in houses of brick, stone and stucco, many built in the course of the eighteenth century. The wide street rose gently westward towards the prominent hill on which Stowey's long-vanished castle had stood, and a Quantock stream, which drove the Stowey corn mill, flowed through a deep stone gutter on the street's southern side.

Architecturally, as in other ways, this pleasing street scene was dominated by an elegant seven-bay house in red Quantock sandstone. It had been built earlier in the century, and by 1794 was the home of Henry Poole's uncle, Thomas Poole the elder, an 'irritable, arbitrary old man' whose bad temper owed only a little to his sufferings from the gout.[20] Though Mrs Poole, gentle-natured and tolerant, made up in part for her disagreeable husband, most who visited the Castle Street house were attracted there by neither of the elder Pooles, but by their son, another Thomas. Such was certainly the case that summer day in 1794, when Henry Poole, with his two poetical companions, at last arrived at his cousin's door.

Thomas Poole the younger had been born into comfortable West Somerset obscurity in 1765, and gave little sign to those who met him for the first time of the great gifts of character and intellect which he possessed. When Thomas De Quincey visited Poole in 1807, he found a 'stout plain-looking farmer', and discovered only later that beyond the plain exterior, the proudly-maintained West Country accent, and the abrupt manner was a man of wide culture and fervently liberal viewpoint, and one who, like Coleridge himself, possessed a remarkable capacity for making friends. Those qualities owed little to the opportunities provided by formal schooling or family background: the Pooles had been tanners in the Stowey area since at least the early eighteenth century, and Tom Poole's father, the eldest of four gifted brothers, ran a large and thriving tanning business from his Castle Street home. He sneered at Tom's bookish

Tom Poole's house
in Castle Street,
Nether Stowey

Tom Poole (1765–
1837) in middle age

tastes, and denied him the education which would better have suited his intelligence and his inclinations. Instead, the elder Poole apprenticed his son at an early age to the tanning trade, the younger showing his resentment by 'ostentatious inattention' to the work of the tanyard and a steady devotion to his books.[21]

If at first Tom Poole's knowledge as a practical tanner suffered in consequence, his commercial acumen and persuasive eloquence did not. In 1790 a great meeting of tanners held in London elected him to speak for them to the prime minister, William Pitt, concerning the distressed state of the tanning trade; and in 1793 he wrote to parliament on behalf of Bristol tanners to suggest remedies for the scarcity of the oak bark used in tanning. His introduction to the greater world during his London visit was important in shaping his liberal sympathies, and when he returned to Stowey in March 1791, his relatives were shocked to find him overflowing with French Revolutionary politics as well as other democratic heresies. By 1794 his letters were being opened by the government, who were said to regard him as 'the most dangerous person in the county of Somerset'.[22] Events would in due course moderate his view of the French experiment, but Poole, in spite of hostility, never abandoned his intelligent radicalism or his strong social conscience. Remembered now for his friendships with Coleridge, Wordsworth, and Humphry Davy, as central to his biography was the fact recorded by his Stowey epitaph, that he remained the 'enlightened Friend of the Poor'.

Coleridge's first meeting with Tom Poole lasted less than a day, but in that short time Coleridge was expansive both on the subject of himself and his plans for the future. He spoke with all his habitual power of his recent follies – 'abberations from prudence' as he called them – and of his resolve now 'to be as sober and rational as his most sober friends could wish'. He discussed religion and politics, leaving no room for doubt that not only was he 'a Unitarian, if not a Deist', but also 'a Democrat, to the utmost extent of the word'. And he described in detail his hopes for Pantisocracy. Poole, as one who had already thought of emigrating to America, listened sympathetically; but he saw at once that the scheme could never succeed, remarking to a friend that however perfectible human nature might be, it was 'not yet perfect enough' for Pantisocracy. Poole was as quick to recognize, however, that Coleridge himself was someone of 'splendid abilities', and before the day was over, the two very different men had established a lasting friendship. Coleridge – mercurial, brilliant, and prodigiously well read – opened to Poole the world of thought and learning he had longed to discover since boyhood. Poole offered in return the benevolent strength and practicality which Coleridge was soon to value so greatly.[23]

The meeting at the Castle Street house was decisive in the lives of both Poole and Coleridge, and was also, though by accident, instantly notorious in the little

Marshmills in Over Stowey, the home of Tom Poole's cousins

39

The Revd John
Poole (1771–1858),
Tom Poole's cousin
and boyhood friend

world of Stowey. Soon after midday Tom Poole and his brother Richard decided to take their interesting visitors on a short walk to the farmhouse called Marshmills in Over Stowey, home of a large tribe of Poole cousins who were almost a second family to Tom and Richard: among them were Penelope Poole, 'a beautiful, dark-eyed girl'[24] who would never return Tom Poole's love for her (he died unmarried), and John Poole, an Oxford fellow and later the rector of Enmore, who was Tom Poole's friend and companion from childhood. John Poole was a man of high Tory opinions, and the motive for introducing him to Coleridge and Southey can only have been mischievous. John Poole, as he recorded in his Latin journal, was predictably scandalized:

> About one o'clock, Tom Poole and his brother Richard, Henry Poole and two young men, friends of his, come in. These two strangers, I understand, had left Cambridge, and had walked nearly all through Wales. One is an undergraduate of Oxford, the other of Cambridge. Each of them was shamefully hot with Democratic rage as regards politics, and Infidel as to religion. I was extremely indignant.[25]

John Poole's temper cannot have been improved when he announced the news of Robespierre's execution, reported in that day's *Western Flying Post*, and prompted from Southey the histrionic cry, 'I had rather have heard of the death of my own father.' In the evening John Reeks, the drunken rector of Aisholt, called at Marshmills to join the chorus of indignation, having met Tom Poole's visitors back at Stowey. There, it seems, the talk had become surpassingly outrageous, and by the time the brief visit came to an end, it was assured of its place in the folklore of the Poole family: John Poole was still recalling it half a century later. The inhabitants of Stowey, for their part, were already passing judgement as Coleridge, Southey, and Henry Poole set off on the road back to Shurton.[26]

☆

In a West Country summer whose consequences were to stay with Coleridge for the rest of his life the most significant event was yet to come. Returning to Bristol from Shurton, he and Southey stopped again at Mrs Southey's house in Westgate Buildings, Bath, and as before found Sarah Fricker there to greet them. The 'epidemic delusion' of Pantisocratic brotherhood had perhaps never been more powerful than at that moment, life on the banks of the Susquehannah never a more siren prospect, and a conversation which began by Coleridge asking Sarah if she would write to him when he returned to Cambridge led quickly to a proposal of marriage, which she accepted. The date was probably 20 or 21 August 1794.[27]

Westgate Buildings, Bath, the home of Mrs Margaret Southey

Southey wrote long afterwards that he was astonished at this turn of events, since Coleridge, such a short time before, had talked of being 'deeply in love with a certain Mary Evans';[28] Coleridge, on the other hand, was later to blame Southey for having persuaded him into marriage against his will. Both were probably guilty of rewriting the history of their true feelings, and it seems clear, at least, that Coleridge's proposal to Sarah Fricker was his own impulsive decision. In the fever of Pantisocracy, he needed no persuasion.

On 2 September Coleridge parted from Southey in Bristol – Southey said it was 'like the losing a limb' – and began a characteristically slow and interrupted progress back to Cambridge for what would prove to be his final term. As Southey was writing next day of a future which opened to him 'a smiling prospect', and of his hopes for 'the purest happiness Man can ever experience', the summer was already at an end.[29]

Somerset in winter: the beach at Kilve near Nether Stowey, later to become the 'favorite seat' of Coleridge and Wordsworth

Chapter Three

BRISTOL AND CLEVEDON

On the morning after his return to Jesus College, Coleridge paused to look about the room from which he had been absent since June, and to record his state of mind in a letter to Southey:

> My God! how tumultuous are the movements of my Heart – Since I quitted this room what and how important Events have been evolved! America! Southey! Miss Fricker! – Yes – Southey – you are right – Even Love is the creature of strong Motive – I certainly love her.[1]

It was an almost convincing affirmation of his feelings for Sara (as Coleridge would henceforward write her name) and his fervour for Pantisocracy certainly showed no decline in the coming weeks. News of Pantisocracy had reached Cambridge before him, where at first it was the cause of disbelieving mirth. By late October, however, it had become the 'universal Topic' in a more serious sense, and on one occasion was expounded by Coleridge in a conversation lasting six hours. At the end of it, his system was declared 'impregnable'.[2]

Already the strains in his relationship with Southey were becoming evident. Letters to Bath and Bristol arrived too seldom and erratically to satisfy the punctilious Southey, who deplored most of all the lack of communication with Sara. To Southey this suggested a disturbing want of seriousness in an engaged man. The doubts maturing in Coleridge's own mind concerning events that summer blossomed alarmingly at the end of September. A letter from Mary Evans, possibly written at George Coleridge's suggestion, begged him to give up his plans for emigration, and addressed him with painful tenderness as 'her best-beloved Brother'. The unexpected shock of this letter produced in Coleridge a 'waking Night-mair of Spirits', and brought a sudden realization of the true state of his feelings for Sara: he felt nothing at all. But, as he assured Southey on 21 October, he was resolved to be true to his word, even as he contemplated a future with 'her, whom I do not love – but whom by every tie of Reason and Honor I ought to love'.[3]

Southey himself had just suffered an unpleasant shock of a different kind. On 17 October the formidable Miss Tyler turned Southey out of doors on College Green, Bristol, having learnt, rather late in the day, of his plans for emigration,

43

Sara Coleridge
(1770–1845), from a
miniature by Matilda
Betham, 1809

and worse, of his intended marriage. 'I attempted to reason, but in vain,' he wrote soon after, having been forced to walk through a rainy night to his mother's house in Bath, his pockets empty, but his 'self approbation' undiminished.[4]

The letter from Mary Evans, and some stridently critical letters from his brothers, left Coleridge paralysed by indecision and self-accusation as the year drew to a close. He wrote to Mary admitting the 'ardent attachment' he had so long felt for her, and asked her to confirm a rumour that she too was now engaged. To be certain that his love was hopeless would, he thought, bring him new strength of purpose. Mary's confirmation of her intended marriage reached Coleridge just before Christmas, and he replied at once in a letter which was his brave and gentle farewell.[5]

'Mark you, Southey! – *I will do my Duty*,' he wrote from London five days later, as he steeled himself for his promised return to Bristol and the renewal of his relationship with Sara. But Coleridge never arrived, and early in January the now beleaguered Southey decided that his endlessly procrastinating friend must be *brought* back from London. Southey looked for him first at the Salutation and Cat in Newgate Street, where the landlord had given Coleridge free quarters because his conversation was so good for trade. Eventually, however, he was traced to new lodgings at the Angel Inn nearby, and shortly afterwards, in spite of protests, was safely on board the Bath coach, with Southey standing guard.[6]

Pantisocracy had not emerged unharmed from the weeks of separation. Despite intense poetical activity by both men, money to finance Pantisocracy had simply not been found, and almost Southey's first words on discovering Coleridge were to announce that he had abandoned immediate hopes of emigration in favour of a new scheme for setting up a trial community on a farm in Wales. Coleridge was dismayed: 'For God's sake – my dear Fellow – tell me what we are to gain by taking a Welch Farm?' But he fell in with Southey's plans, none the less, and agreed that in the meantime they must live frugally in Bristol and earn money. By February 1795 three Pantisocratic brothers – Coleridge, Southey, and George Burnett – were settled together in lodgings at 25 College Street, Bristol, very close to the cathedral, and to Southey's Aunt Tyler. The Susquehannah could not have been farther off.[7]

Lithograph of Bristol from Clifton Wood. After a painting by W.J. Muller, 1835. Brandon Hill and the cathedral appear left of centre; St Mary Redcliffe, with its truncated spire, is on the right

Coleridge became almost at once a leader of Bristol's vigorous and combative intellectual life, in which the radical sympathies of a prosperous nonconformist community confronted the conservatism of wealthy merchants and professional men. By late February he had already 'endeavored to disseminate Truth' in the form of three political lectures, the first two delivered at the Corn Market in Wine Street, the third in a vacant house on Castle Green. The fury aroused by his anti-Pitt eloquence was at once frightening and flattering to his vanity. He found himself being harried by 'Mobs and Mayors, Blockheads and Brickbats, Placards and Press gangs', and more seriously threatened by 'two or three uncouth and unbrained Automata'. During his third lecture the crowd outside the house was scarcely prevented from attacking it to get at the 'damn'd Jacobine' inside. Coleridge had worked intensely, under Southey's close scrutiny, to prepare the lectures, and had written the first at a single sitting between midnight and breakfast-time on the day it was delivered. Further lectures by both Coleridge and Southey were to follow, those which Coleridge delivered including one attacking the slave trade and another concerning the Hair Powder Tax (later to become the improbable subject of his first sermon); and at the end of June he began a series at the Assembly Coffee House on the Quay comparing the English Civil War and the French Revolution.[8]

If the radical tendency of his lectures brought him enemies, it was the new friends he was making who were to prove more important. Among them were Josiah Wade, a radical Bristol tradesman, and John Prior Estlin, a Unitarian minister with whose religious opinions Coleridge's own were beginning increasingly to coincide. At an uncertain date between late August and late September there was also a first meeting with a virtually unknown poet and radical called William Wordsworth, two years Coleridge's senior. Wordsworth was the guest in Bristol of a wealthy sugar merchant, John Pretor Pinney, whose sons had recently befriended the poet, and it may have been at the Pinney town house in Great George Street that the meeting with Coleridge took place. That, at least, is the unreliable tradition. Wordsworth himself recalled in old age that he had first met Coleridge, together with Southey, and Edith and Sara Fricker, at 'a lodging in Bristol'. On that evidence, 25 College Street, or possibly the Fricker house on Redcliffe Hill, would seem the more likely setting, though wherever the meeting occurred, its consequences in the private and artistic lives of both men were greater than either could even dimly have foreseen. Wordsworth was quick to take the measure of his new acquaintance. 'Coleridge was at Bristol part of the time I was there,' he wrote in October. 'I saw but little of him. I wished indeed to have seen more – his talent appears to me very great.'[9]

☆

Coleridge's relationship with Sara in these months was developing in unexpected ways. He discovered soon after his return to the city that she had refused two

S. T. COLERIDGE,

Propoſes to give in SIX LECTURES a COMPARATIVE VIEW of the

ENGLISH REBELLION under CHARLES the Firſt,

AND THE

FRENCH REVOLUTION.

The SUBJECTS of the propoſed LECTURES are,

I.

THE diſtinguiſhing Marks of the French and Engliſh Character with their probable Cauſes. The national Circumſtances precurſive to (1) the Engliſh Rebellion, (2) the French Revolution.

II.

The Liberty of the Preſs. Literature—its revolutionary Powers. Compariſon of the Engliſh with the French political Writers at the time of the ſeveral Revolutions. MILTON. SYDNEY. HARRINGTON. BRISSOT. SEYEYES. MIRABEAU. THOMAS PAYNE.

III.

The fanaticiſm of the (1) Engliſh, and (2) French Revolutioniſts. Engliſh Sectaries. French Parties:—Feuillans, Girondiſts, Faction of Hebert, Jacobins, Moderants, Royaliſts.

IV.

1. Characters of Charles I$^{st.}$ and Louis the XVI$^{th.}$ 2. Of Louis the XIV$^{th.}$ and the preſent Empreſs of Ruſſia. 3. Lives and Characters of *Eſſex* and *Fayette.*

V.

OLIVER CROMWELL, and ROBESPIERRE.—CARDINAL MAZARINE, and WILLIAM PITT.— DUNDAS, and BARRERE.

VI.

On Revolution in general—its moral Cauſes, and probable effects on the revolutionary People, and ſurrounding Nations.

It is intended, that the Lectures ſhould be given once a Week, on TUESDAY EVENINGS, at Eight o'Clock, at the ASSEMBLY COFFEE HOUSE, on the QUAY.—The firſt Lecture, on Tueſday, June 23, 1795. As the Author wiſhes to inſure an Audience adequate to the Expences of the Room, he has prepared Subſcription Tickets for the whole courſe, price SIX SHILLINGS, which may be had at the Lecture Room, and at Mr. REED's, Bookſeller, Wine-Street.

BIGGS, PRINTER.

Notice advertising Coleridge's lectures comparing the English Civil War and the French Revolution, 1795

The town house of
the Pinney family in
Great George Street,
Bristol. It was here
that some of the
early meetings of
Coleridge and
Wordsworth
probably took place

William Wordswor
(1770–1851). Pencil
and chalk drawing
by Robert Hancock
1798

The bridge leading into Bristol High Street, 1829

offers of marriage – one from a wealthy suitor – on the strength of the promise made to him at Bath, and that she continued to love him 'with an affection to the ardor of which my Deserts bear no proportion'. The deadening sense of obligation with which Coleridge had returned to Bristol was now swiftly transformed, until, as a 'neutral spectator' (perhaps Cottle) told Thomas De Quincey, 'if ever in his life he had seen a man under deep fascination, and what he would have called desperately in love, Coleridge, in relation to Miss F——, was that man'.[10]

At the same time, friendship with Robert Southey was in further steep decline. Coleridge became aware soon after their lectures began that Southey's manner had grown 'cold and gloomy', and that he had started to back away from the principles of Pantisocracy. In part, Southey's changed manner reflected his desperate irritation with someone whose procrastinating habits had become unignorable in the cramped spaces of 25 College Street (Coleridge admitted to Southey that 'you sate down and wrote – I used to saunter about and think what I should write'). But more important were Southey's fundamental doubts concerning the likely success of Pantisocracy in any form. Coleridge remembered with bewilderment the occasions of some more memorable disagreements on the subject: during a strawberry party at Long Ashton; crossing the bridge below Bristol High Street after visiting the Fricker family; on a two-day excursion to Chepstow and Tintern with Joseph Cottle, Edith and Sara, during which, with poetical appropriateness, they all got lost in pitch darkness above Tintern Abbey and Southey 'marched on like a pillar of strength, with a lady pressing on each arm'. The final breach grew from Southey's good fortune in being offered an annuity of £160 during the summer of 1795. Thereupon Southey announced that, Pantisocrat or no, his private resources were his own, and that on the Welsh farm each person should manage his own affairs. 'In short,' Coleridge wrote bitterly near the end of the year, 'we were to commence Partners in a petty Farming Trade. This was the Mouse of which the Mountain Pantisocracy was at last safely delivered!' The two men ceased for a time even to acknowledge one another in the street; and though they later resumed formal courtesies, close friendship was dead. 'You have left a large void in my Heart,' Coleridge wrote in November. 'I know no man big enough to fill it.'[11]

Marriage to Sara had become by late summer not only a longed-for end in the midst of disillusionment, but an increasingly urgent necessity. The unchaperoned freedom with which she and her sister had gone about the city with their prospective husbands had given rise to the 'hostile breath of rumour', and had encouraged a general belief that 'Pantisocracy meant a system of things which dispensed with the marriage-tie'. Coleridge and Sara fixed their wedding for early October, and in the meantime began looking for a home. The cottage which they eventually discovered at Clevedon, on the Somerset coast south of Bristol, was not quite the 'honeymoon cottage' it has often been called. Coleridge viewed it rather as another home for Pantisocracy, even though his companions and fellow believers were reduced now to Sara herself and George Burnett. (His concern for the floundering Burnett showed Coleridge at his best during these months: Southey abandoned Burnett; Coleridge stayed loyal to him, even though the two men were not special friends.)[12]

The cottage – which was probably not the cottage now bearing a commemorative tablet – lay in a wooded 'Valley of Seclusion' at the west end of Clevedon, close to the parish church where Arthur Hallam is buried. Coleridge and Sara, in further disregard of the proprieties, first stayed at the cottage on about 20 August 1795, over a month before their marriage. They were deeply in love, and the strength of their feelings for one another, together with the great natural beauty of the 'green and woody' landscape which surrounded them, induced in Coleridge a depth of contentment he would rarely find again. The immediate result was the short love poem which he later revised and expanded as 'The

The cottage at Clevedon traditionally, and probably erroneously, associated with Coleridge, *c.* 1840

Eolian Harp', but which even in its original form showed him speaking in a manner now distinctively his own. With his 'pensive Sara' leaning on his arm, he writes with conversational ease and descriptive felicity of their cottage overgrown with jasmine and myrtle, of the scents drifting from a neighbouring bean-field, and the 'stilly murmur' of the distant sea. To a revision of the poem published in 1803 he added the lines, 'Methinks, it should have been impossible/Not to love all things in a World like this', his words seeming to carry the weight of his later regret that his unclouded times with Sara were so quickly over. But for the moment, the prospect of marriage to a woman he loved, and of life together in a place of exquisite beauty, seemed to offer the stability and direction he never ceased to crave in his personal life. 'Domestic Happiness is the greatest of things sublunary,' he had written to Southey earlier in August, 'and of things celestial it is perhaps impossible for unassisted Man to believe any thing greater.' Now, for the first time, domestic happiness seemed within his own reach.[13]

In September he returned, after more than a year, to visit Henry Poole at Shurton Court, and to renew his friendship with Tom Poole, now master of the Castle Street house since the death of his father in July. Tom Poole, who had nursed his father devotedly at the end, was in low spirits, but was as instantly captivated by his visitor as he had been at their first meeting. He addressed Coleridge, with more enthusiasm than skill, in a poem which begins 'Hail to thee Coleridge, youth of various powers!', and which expresses in its stilted, conventional way, something of the electrifying effect produced by Coleridge's passionate eloquence on any sympathetic listener. Coleridge's themes were the predictable ones: the rift with Southey, the folly of the world, his love for Sara, and Pantisocracy. Even the unsympathetic could not but be impressed, and when Charlotte Poole, Tom's cousin, met Coleridge at Marshmills that month, she mingled her disapproval with admiration, setting him down in her journal as 'a young man of brilliant understanding, great eloquence, desperate fortune, democratick principles, and entirely led away by the feelings of the moment'.[14]

Another and better poem, written by Coleridge himself, also resulted from his September journey. At Shurton, a letter reached him in which Sara evidently wrote sadly of the growing coolness in her relations with Edith and Southey. Imagining his Sara 'all oppressed with gloom', Coleridge's spontaneous reply was a poem set in the descriptive frame of an evening visit to Shurton Bars, the coastal area lying beyond a rich tract of open fields to the north of Shurton Court. The coast at Shurton Bars shelves more gently to the sea than at many points farther west, and in the eighteenth century still provided a landing-place for infrequent trading vessels which brought coal from Wales for coastal lime-kilns and West Somerset hearths. But in general, it was a place bereft of human

The Somerset coast at Shurton Bars

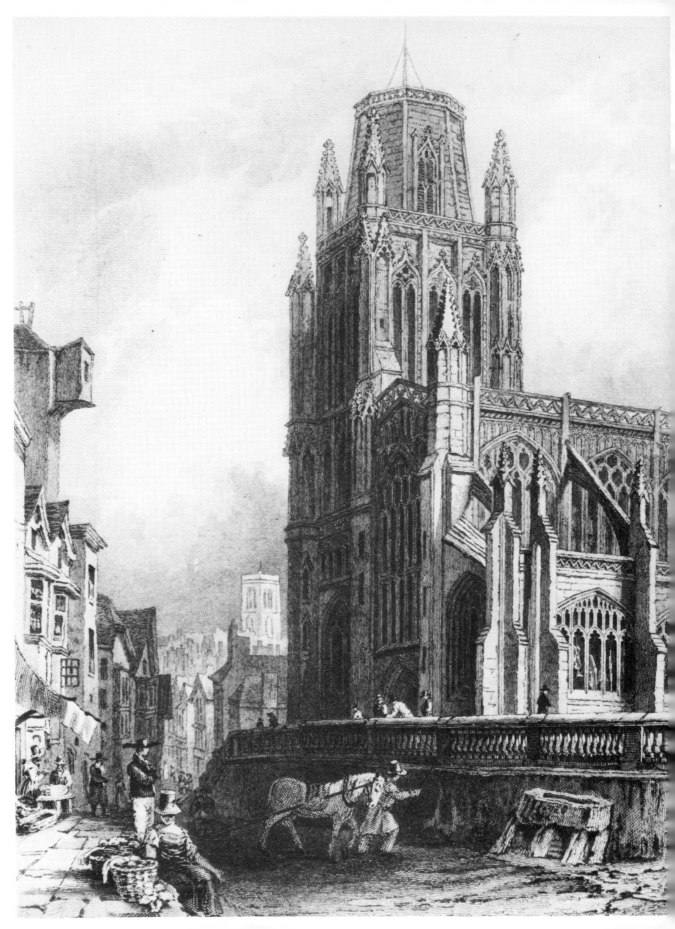

activity, where a grey sea rolled unattended on to sand and shingle, and the only house was an abandoned shell (whose ruins still survive). Such a setting, as Coleridge acknowledges in the poem, he might once have sought out to echo the mood of a 'sad gloom-pamper'd Man'; but now his descriptions of the sea breeze moaning through the house, the thunder of the 'onward-surging tides' and the watchfire shining out from Flat Holm in the Bristol Channel, are powerfully transformed by the central fact of his love for Sara, and become part of a vast natural counterpoint to intimate and far from gloomy thoughts. 'Lines Written at Shurton Bars' shows Coleridge progressing rapidly from the bland natural description contained in poems such as the one he had written in May 'while climbing the left ascent of Brockley Coomb', and opens the way to the 'Conversation Poems' of the following three years, where feelings of friendship and love – for Charles Lamb, the Wordsworths, his infant son Hartley – stand in close and creative relationship with luminous descriptions of nature.[15]

☆

On the morning of Sunday 4 October 1795 Samuel Taylor Coleridge and Sara Fricker were finally married in the vast cathedral-like spaces of St Mary Redcliffe Church in Bristol, close to the Fricker house on Redcliffe Hill. Mrs Fricker, despite her family's opposition to the match, condescended to be a witness, as did Coleridge's new friend Josiah Wade, and the only 'tinge of melancholy to the solemn Joy' was provided by the thought that this was Chatterton's church, where, in a room above the north porch, the boy poet had supposedly found his poetic forgeries. Five weeks later, on 13 November, Southey and Edith Fricker were secretly married in the same church, Southey setting off almost immediately afterwards to spend six months with his uncle in Portugal, leaving Edith behind.[16]

Coleridge and Sara began their married life more conventionally, and within a few days he was writing in enraptured terms to Tom Poole from their 'comfortable Cot' in Clevedon: 'the prospect around us is perhaps more *various* than any in the kingdom – Mine Eye gluttonizes. – The Sea – the distant Islands! – the opposite Coasts! – I shall assuredly write Rhymes – let the nine Muses prevent it, if they can.' For the moment, however, domestic considerations were more pressing. The most notable household items they had thought to bring with them were evidently 'some old *Prints*', and almost at once Joseph Cottle was called upon to supply further essentials, including a kettle, a pair of candlesticks, a tin dustpan, a cheese toaster, two large tin spoons, a keg of porter, and a Bible. Cottle obliged his impractical friends with his habitual amused indulgence, and having sent Coleridge 'all that he had required, and more', rode down to Clevedon the following day to pay his respects in person. He was happily surprised to find that the cottage did indeed live up to Coleridge's estimate of it, possessing 'every thing that heart could desire', including a small flower garden

The Church of St Mary Redcliffe, Bristol, 1829

55

and a climbing rose which Coleridge was soon to commemorate in verse. Only wallpaper for the whitewashed parlour seemed, at least in Cottle's opinion, to be lacking, and he accordingly sent an upholsterer down to Clevedon a few days later to paste up some 'sprightly paper'.[17]

Sea-bathing, walks on the steep coastal hills above the cottage – where Coleridge could watch the sunbeams 'dance, like diamonds, on the main' – and the continuing assurance of Sara's love, were enough to quell any restless dissatisfaction while the last of a mild autumn remained. Coleridge even felt some confidence that his writing could sustain them both in their new life: Cottle, in a further act of generosity, had offered him a guinea and a half for every one hundred lines of poetry he produced, and faithfully honoured the bargain in April of the following year when he published *Poems on Various Subjects*, Coleridge's first major collection.[18]

But Coleridge soon discovered the shortcomings of Clevedon, and especially the inconvenient distance separating it from his literary friends in Bristol, and from the indispensable Bristol City Library. Having been reduced now to travelling on foot, he could not make the return journey to Bristol in a day, and Sara too often found herself left lonely and uneasy in a cottage whose attractions were not increased by the coming of winter, or by neighbours who were 'a little too tattling and inquisitive'. When, in November, Coleridge was persuaded by his Bristol friends that he should return permanently to the city, he expressed sadness at leaving Clevedon, but probably felt relatively little, even though the only home available to him and Sara was in cramped quarters in Mrs Fricker's house. Coleridge rationalized the departure in his poem 'Reflections on having left a Place of Retirement', asking whether it was right that he should live in beauty and solitude while his 'unnumber'd brethren toil'd and bled' in the greater world. The grandiose question hid Coleridge's simple discovery that neither natural beauty nor loving domesticity could replace his need for intellectual stimulation and a creed to hold to and to preach. While he was casting a regretful backward glance to the 'dear Cot' at Clevedon, the familiar towers and spires of Bristol already loomed invitingly.[19]

Bristol, like much of England, was in political turmoil when Coleridge reached it in November. Crop failure in the previous year and the debilitating effects of war with France had brought national scarcity and popular protest by the end of 1795, and in London, King George had been lucky to escape when his coach was attacked by stone-throwing crowds crying 'Bread! Peace! No Pitt!' The government replied with the introduction of the 'Two Bills', against seditious meetings and treasonable practices, and successfully aroused the contending arguments of conservatives and radicals throughout the land.

A meeting at Bristol Guildhall on 17 November was called to congratulate the king on his escape, but attracted as well a large group who wished to implore him to end the war. One voice in particular repeatedly called out 'Mr Mayor! Mr Mayor!' in an attempt to be heard, and then embarked on 'the most elegant, the most pathetic, and the most sublime Address that was ever heard, perhaps, within the walls of that building'. The voice was Coleridge's, arguing that although the war had been costly to the rich, it had left them much; 'but a PENNY taken from the pocket of a poor man might deprive him of a dinner'.[20]

That month Coleridge kept up the radical cry by publishing some of his Bristol lectures from earlier in the year, under the title *Conciones ad Populum*, and in late December he embarked on an altogether bolder enterprise. At a meeting in the Rummer Tavern (which still exists in rebuilt form a few doors from Cottle's former bookshop) he was persuaded by 'sundry Philanthropists' and opponents of the war to begin publication of a periodical to be called the *Watchman*. Cottle

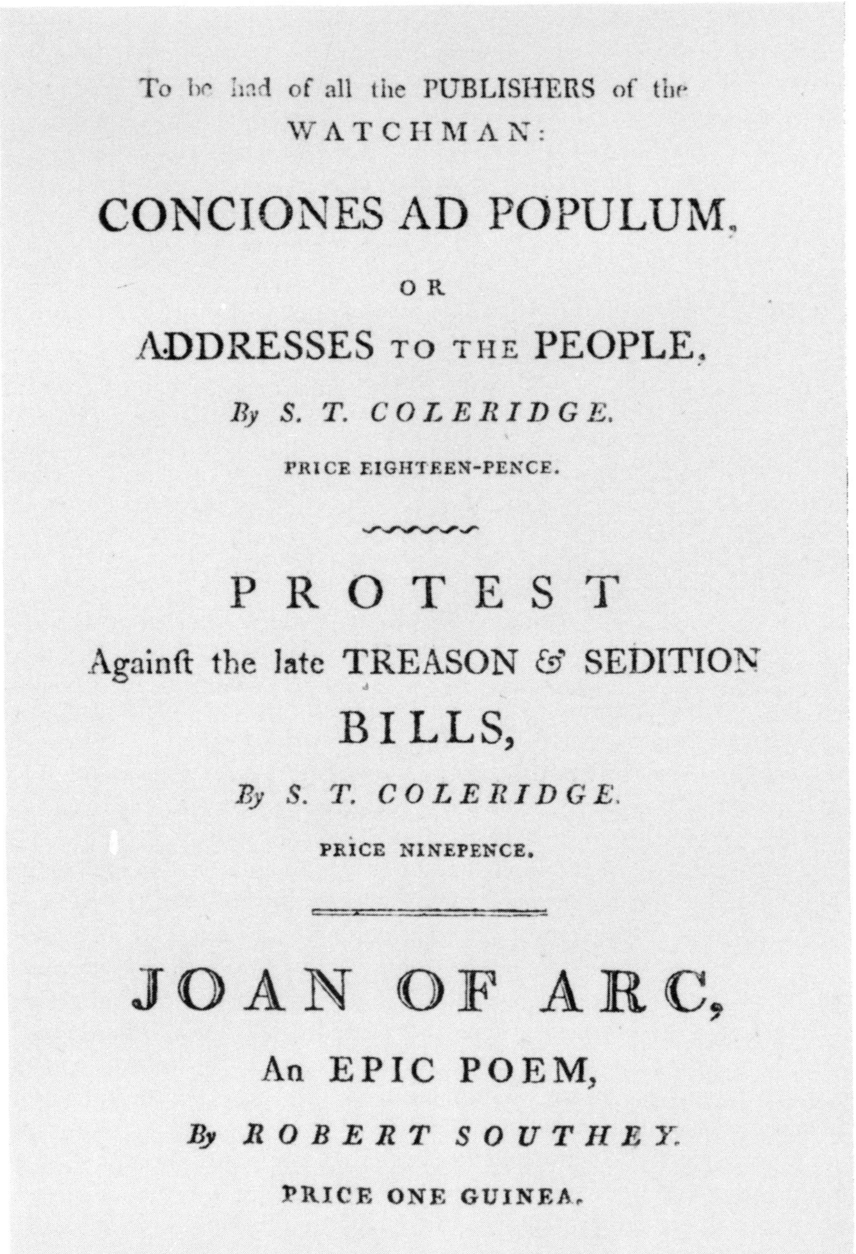

To be had of all the PUBLISHERS of the
WATCHMAN:

CONCIONES AD POPULUM,

OR

ADDRESSES TO THE PEOPLE,

By S. T. COLERIDGE.

PRICE EIGHTEEN-PENCE.

~~~~

PROTEST

Againſt the late TREASON & SEDITION

BILLS,

By S. T. COLERIDGE.

PRICE NINEPENCE.

JOAN OF ARC,

An EPIC POEM,

By ROBERT SOUTHEY.

PRICE ONE GUINEA.

Notice advertising
Coleridge's *Conciones
ad Populum* and
Southey's epic poem,
Joan of Arc, 1796

thought that Coleridge, of all men, was 'least qualified to display periodical industry', and many friends in the city were equally doubtful. But they gave him their support, none the less, and the first issue, containing political reports, original essays, poetry, and reviews, was announced for the beginning of March, the aim of the publication being, as Coleridge modestly explained, 'to proclaim the State of the Political Atmosphere, and preserve Freedom and her Friends from the attacks of Robbers and Assassins!!'[21]

Cottle and others succeeded in finding over three hundred subscribers for the *Watchman* in Bristol alone. But many more were needed, and in early January Coleridge set off to publicize the new venture on a tour of the Midlands, recording an eventful journey with comic gusto both in his letters at the time and almost twenty years later in the *Biographia Literaria*. He talked religion with the great Erasmus Darwin in Derby, preached to sometimes vast congregations from Unitarian pulpits – 'my *Sermons* spread a sort of sanctity over my *Sedition*' – and returned in triumph to Bristol with the names of several hundred new subscribers.[22] His idealistic and high-spirited mood came back to him in memory when in 1815, almost his darkest time, the *Biographia* was written:

O! never can I remember those days with either shame or regret. For I was most sincere, most disinterested! My opinions were indeed in many and most important points erroneous; but my heart was single. Wealth, rank, life itself then seemed cheap to me, compared with the interests of (what I believed to be) the truth, and the will of my maker.[23]

The drudgery of compiling the *Watchman* to peremptory deadlines, and with little help, quickly evoked very different feelings in Coleridge. The printer was careless, George Burnett a forgetful and utterly incompetent assistant, and all the time Sara's groans of pain were announcing the early stages of a difficult pregnancy. Nor were readers much happier. Cottle wrote that 'a feeling of disappointment prevailed early and pretty generally, amongst the subscribers', and when in the second issue Coleridge included a rather too satirical essay on fasting, he lost goodwill alarmingly.[24]

The *Watchman* survived until 13 May 1796, when the tenth and final issue appeared, Coleridge leaving his readers with explanations, regrets, and the words of the prophet, 'O Watchman! thou hast watched in vain!' To the man on whose support he would now increasingly depend, he wrote a little before the end, 'It is not pleasant, Thomas Poole! to have worked 14 weeks for nothing – *for nothing* – nay – to have given the Public in addition to that toil five & 40 pounds!' Much of the substantial loss which Coleridge suffered was borne by the uncomplaining and insufficiently thanked Cottle, whose verdict on the *Watchman* was brief and to the point. 'It was', he said, 'a losing concern, altogether.'[25]

☆

Coleridge found it difficult to accept failure quite so dispassionately. The publication in April of *Poems on Various Subjects*, its preface written at the last moment in Cottle's bookshop, was a genuine cause for satisfaction and received enthusiastic reviews. But Coleridge soon found himself adrift once more on a sea of self-doubt, without employment of any kind, and without money. The troubles which surrounded him were not just his own. On a stormy night at the beginning of May he watched by the bedside of his brother-in-law, Robert Lovell, as he lay dying from a putrid fever, and tried to comfort Lovell's young wife Mary, who was listening frantically to her husband's 'loud, deep, unintermitted groans' during his final hours. At the same time, Coleridge's mother-in-law, Mrs Fricker, also seemed on the point of death at the house in Oxford Street, Kingsdown, that he had just found for Sara and himself on the north side of the city. (In the event Mrs Fricker survived until 1809, dying on the same November day as Coleridge's own mother.) Weighed down by a burden of 'domestic Sorrows & external disappointments' that threatened to overwhelm him, he turned once again to Tom Poole – 'my dear, very dear Friend' – and on about 15 May set off in the carrier's van for Stowey. He stayed a fortnight, and during that time dined memorably on honey pie, made an even more unfavourable impression at Marshmills, and no doubt spent long hours talking in Poole's garden arbour, 'an Elysium', as he called it, in which he had already recited many of his recent poems.[26]

There was much to discuss, including Tom Poole's proposal, in the end gratefully accepted, that he and a few friends should supply Coleridge with an annuity of £35 or £40 as a 'trifling mark of their esteem, gratitude and admiration'. But neither £40 a year nor the financial kindnesses of other friends were enough to rescue Coleridge from the need for hard decisions. While Poole was urging him to remain true above all to poetry, Coleridge still had no sense of a purely poetic, or even literary, vocation, and for the moment could offer only two vague plans for the future, 'the first impracticable – the second not likely to succeed': he could 'make a portly Quarto' by translating all the works of Schiller, then set up a school at 100 guineas a head, or he could 'abjure Politics & carnal literature' altogether and become a dissenting parson. He left Stowey with his thinking no farther advanced, but with an ever-growing admiration for Tom Poole and affection for his home. 'Dear Gutter of Stowey!' he wrote at Bridgwater while he waited distractedly for the carrier. 'Were I transported to Italian Plains, and lay by the side of a streamlet that murmured thro' an Orange-Grove, I would think of thee. . . .'[27]

Other friends tried to help. Dr Thomas Beddoes, a Bristol physician at Hotwells, told him of an opportunity to write for the *Morning Chronicle* in London, and Coleridge, with a heavy heart, almost accepted the editor's 'very handsome offer'. 'If I go,' he wrote to Poole, 'farewell Philosophy! Farewell, the Muse! Farewell, my literary Fame!' Plans in August to become tutor to the children of a Derbyshire widow called Elizabeth Evans quickly foundered

Castle Street, Nether Stowey, *c.* 1920. The cars stand outside Tom Poole's house, and the 'dear gutter of Stowey' is visible on the right-hand side of the road

(although Mrs Evans greatly admired Coleridge), and by the beginning of September he was speaking in decided terms of opening a day-school in Derby. 'In all human probability,' he wrote, 'I shall settle at Derby in November.' Such a note of finality was not, however, to be relied upon, and he was soon writing to Poole of racking doubts and of 'dim & huddled' feelings. Terrible neuralgic pains which troubled him throughout this period were the mirror of his inward distress, and the large doses of laudanum he took to relieve his symptoms, a portent for the future. By 15 October 1796, almost a month after the birth of his son David Hartley Coleridge, he had at last reached a decision. But the course he now proposed to take amounted, in effect, to a failure to decide, a refusal to make any of the conventional choices available to him, a creative act of cowardice.[28]

He would go to live near Stowey, and Tom Poole.

Chapter Four

'A BEAUTIFUL COUNTRY'

Having reached an ebb of spirits comparable to that which, a year before, had followed his breach with Southey, Coleridge was suddenly filled again with hopes and plans, and at the beginning of November wrote to Tom Poole with a sense of joyful liberation:

> To live in a beautiful country & to inure myself as much as possible to the labors of the field, have been for this year past my dream of the day, my Sigh at midnight – but to enjoy these blessings *near you*, to see you daily, to tell you all my thoughts in their first birth, and to hear your's, to be mingling identities with you, as it were; – the vision-weaving *Fancy* has indeed often pictured such things, but *Hope* never dared whisper a promise![1]

His decision to reject a future of schoolmastering was evidently taken after a brief and desperate visit to Stowey at the end of September. He dreaded most, he said, the physical and mental confinement which teaching seemed to threaten, but had also been greatly affected by the birth of his son. When first he saw Hartley, as a sonnet written soon after memorably records, he felt only sadness, reminded unexpectedly of his own childhood self, and fearful what his son's future might be. It was a momentary thought, quickly dispelled when Sara took Hartley in her arms; but from it crystallized the firm decision that both Hartley and any other children they might have should be spared a city childhood, and be 'bred up from earliest infancy in the simplicity of peasants, their food, dress, and habits completely rustic'. The banks of the Susquehannah lay out of reach as a setting in which to realize this vision; the streams which flowed from the Quantock Hills passed through a landscape which had already begun to seem hardly less desirable.[2]

Coleridge's Somerset household was at first intended to have a touch of Pantisocratic inclusiveness. He would be moving there not only with Sara and the baby, but with Sara's mother, their servant Nanny, and a young man called Charles Lloyd, who had fallen under Coleridge's spell after meeting him in Birmingham. Lloyd had persuaded Coleridge to take him as a pupil at £80 a year; but when his wealthy father, a member of the banking family, insisted that the arrangement could last only for a year, Coleridge's expectation of a regular

The Quantock Hills
seen from West
Quantoxhead, 1791

income suddenly vanished, and Lloyd eventually settled with him as an occasional lodger, not a pupil. Mrs Fricker, for her part, was soon wise enough to discover 'a great aversion to leaving Bristol'.[3]

Not only was the membership of Coleridge's proposed household in doubt for many weeks, but also its exact location. During one of his Somerset visits he had already discovered Adscombe, a hamlet of Over Stowey parish not far from Tom Poole's cousins at Marshmills. It was a place of great beauty and utter seclusion, lying in a sheltered combe on the eastern flanks of the Quantocks. The hamlet consisted of little more than the substantially-built Adscombe Farm, three cottages, and a ruined medieval chapel, probably the original of the chapel in 'The Foster-Mother's Tale' whose leaning wall was propped by a 'huge round beam'.

Adscombe Farm,
Over Stowey

It was in this 'enchanting Situation' that Coleridge at first hoped to obtain a cottage with six acres, the property of Lord Egmont of Enmore Castle. John Cruikshank, Tom Poole's friend and neighbour, promised to get the cottage; but Coleridge was left 'full, yea, crammed with anxieties' as negotiations ground on. 'I am frightened at not hearing from Cruikshanks,' he wrote to Poole at the beginning of November. 'Has Lord Thing a my bob – I forget the animal's name – refused *him* – or has Cruickshanks forgotten *me*?' At first it seemed that the only delay was in making the cottage fit to occupy, and Coleridge wondered whether, until it was ready, there might not be some rooms to spare at Shurton Court. Soon, however, it became clear that Cruikshank had promised more than he could deliver, and after two months of waiting, all hopes of Adscombe were given up.[4]

Desperate in his anxiety to leave Bristol, almost any available house now seemed acceptable to Coleridge so long as it was near Tom Poole. There was only one. It was the decaying thatched cottage known as Gilbard's which stood at the top of Lime Street in Stowey, and which had been occupied until then by a widow called Elizabeth Rendell. Tom Poole suggested it as a last resort, and Coleridge, who remembered the cottage, immediately asked him to take it for a year. (The landlord was Mr Blake, member of a prominent local family.) 'It is not

The City Library,
King Street, Bristol.
Watercolour by
Edward Cashin,
1823

a beauty, to be sure,' Coleridge wrote to Poole on 28 November; 'but it's vicinity to you shall overbalance it's Defects.' Content that all was finally settled, Coleridge was unprepared when his West Country plans were threatened by one further difficulty, raised at the last moment by Tom Poole himself. Poole's letter to Coleridge of about 10 December has not survived, but it was the cause of 'unexpected and most acute pain' and expressed Poole's doubts that the Lime Street cottage could ever be a suitable home. He rashly suggested that, as an alternative to Stowey, Coleridge might like to consider Iron Acton near Bristol, where he could be closer to his city friends. It is not clear whether Poole's motives were merely altruistic, or whether, as seems more likely, he had begun to question the wisdom of having an emotionally dependent and notoriously radical young poet as his neighbour. Coleridge's own feelings, on the other hand, were beyond any doubt. Opening Poole's letter on a visit to Bristol City Library, he began at once to write the first of two wildly intemperate replies: the country round Iron Acton was 'intolerably flat'; Bristol contained no friends of his beyond Cottle and Estlin (Wade was going away); and as for the cottage, he would *make* it do. He and Sara would not want much, and sixteen shillings a week would be enough to keep them, money which Coleridge intended to earn by reviewing. 'Pardon me if I write vehemently,' he apologized disingenuously to Poole in his second letter, adding with more than a hint of picturesque excess:

Mrs Coleridge has observed the workings of my face, while I have been writing; and is intreating to know what is the matter – I dread to shew her your Letter – I dread it. My God! my God! what if she should dare to think, that my most beloved Friend is grown cold towards me!

Coleridge in such cajoling and overwrought spirits was not to be thwarted, and Poole sensibly gave up all further resistance.[5]

On the last day of 1796 Coleridge, Sara and the baby finally left Bristol on their journey west, a wagon following after them loaded high with 'boxes of Books, and Chests of Drawers, & Kitchen-Furniture, & Chairs, and our Bed and Bed-Linen, &c &c'. They had chosen one of the coldest Decembers ever recorded in England to make their journey, and Coleridge, plagued once more with neuralgia and illness, was suffering at the time from a face 'monstrously swoln'. But his mood was calm. He turned from Bristol without regret and entered again the West Somerset landscape of coast and hills over which, very soon, he would become a persistent and delighted explorer. At the same time, he was entering with a new singleness of purpose the creative landscape of his own mind, and sensed already that what he might achieve in the months ahead would surpass anything which had resulted from two very public years in Bristol. 'I am not *fit* for *public* Life,' he wrote from Bristol to his new friend John Thelwall, the radical lecturer; 'yet the Light shall stream to a far distance from the taper in my cottage window'.[6]

Church bells ringing out the old year from the tower at Over Stowey probably formed a distant accompaniment to Coleridge's first night in the Lime Street cottage. His own farewell to 1796 was made in his 'Ode to the Departing Year', a bleak prophecy of war and ruin in which Coleridge renounces his role as public commentator, and dedicates himself to the 'deep Sabbath of meek self-content' he hoped that Stowey, the Quantocks, and Tom Poole would now make possible. But as he and Sara looked about their new home in a winter twilight, they must soon have recognized that the Lime Street cottage would be one major obstacle in the path to contentment of any kind.[7]

Though Gilbard's was not quite so irredeemable a hovel as some have claimed, its shortcomings were plentiful enough. The cottage, which was regularly to shelter four or five inhabitants together with frequent guests, was a tiny building. On the ground floor were two small parlours on either side of an entrance passage, and beyond them a rudimentary kitchen. Above were three correspondingly small bedrooms, two of which looked out on the narrow and often gloomy street. To the defects of a house with little space and less privacy were added general dilapidation, a plague of mice (which Coleridge was too good-natured to set traps for) and a daily flow of traffic past the door on a turnpike road

Coleridge's cottage as it may have appeared early in the nineteenth century. The lattice windows which Hazlitt remembered were replaced by sashes when the Coleridges finally gave up the cottage at the end of 1799

transformed in wet weather to 'an impassable Hog-stye . . . a Slough of Despond'. But worst of all in those first winter days was the cold. 'I can endure cold,' Coleridge had written earlier in December, 'but not a cold room! If we can but contrive to make two rooms *warm*, & *wholesome*, we will laugh in the faces of Gloom & Ill-lookingness.' A dozen yards of cheap green cloth for stopping draughts, and determined efforts to make the chimney draw, overcame the worst effects of the weather, and the generosity of Tom Poole did most of the rest. Sara would always remember gratefully the help he gave at that time 'to render a miserable cottage, an abode of comparative comfort'. Within a few days they were ready to invite Poole to a dinner of roast pork and potatoes – cooked in the baker's oven because the cottage had none that could be used – and at the end of January a letter to John Prior Estlin described with quiet enthusiasm the clear brook which ran before the cottage door, a pretty garden – 'large enough to find us vegetables and employment' – and an orchard lying beyond which was about to become home for some ducks and geese, as well as two pigs. By early February, Coleridge had achieved for the moment something like contented self-sufficiency in both his inward and outward life. 'I never go to Bristol,' he wrote to John Thelwall.

From seven to half past eight I work in my garden; from breakfast till 12 I read

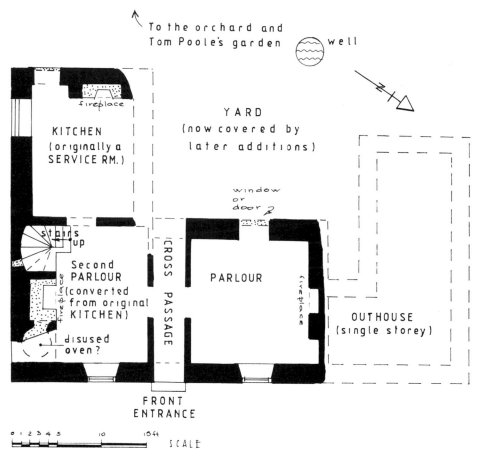

To the orchard and
Tom Poole's garden ◯ well

YARD
(now covered by
later additions)

KITCHEN
(originally a
SERVICE RM.)

fireplace

window
or
door?

stairs
up

Second
PARLOUR
(converted
from original
KITCHEN)

disused
oven?

CROSS
PASSAGE

PARLOUR

fireplace

OUTHOUSE
(single storey)

FRONT
ENTRANCE

0 1 2 3 4 5   10   15ft
SCALE

Ground-floor plan of Coleridge's cottage as it probably appeared in 1797–8. The surviving remnants of the eighteenth-century building are shown in solid black, the parts which have vanished as broken lines. The cottage is essentially of the seventeenth century but was restored in 1800 and greatly enlarged during the second half of the nineteenth century

& compose; then work again – feed the pigs, poultry &c, till two o'clock – after dinner work again till Tea – from Tea till supper *review*. So jogs the day; & I am happy.[8]

That, needless to say, was at best half the story, since Tom Poole's house had immediately become for Coleridge a spacious and comfortable refuge whenever Lime Street grew oppressive. A gate set up by Tom Poole at the bottom of the Lime Street orchard led directly into his own garden, a small secluded area which lay at some distance behind Poole's house in Castle Street and which contained, beneath the shelter of a lime-tree, a jasmine-covered arbour. (A modern bungalow now occupies the site.) From this garden Coleridge could either walk on through Poole's orchard and a 'fine meadow' to the home of his new friends, John and Anna Cruikshank, or he could negotiate Poole's tanyard and its 'Tartarean tan-pits' to reach the Castle Street house itself. The 'great windy

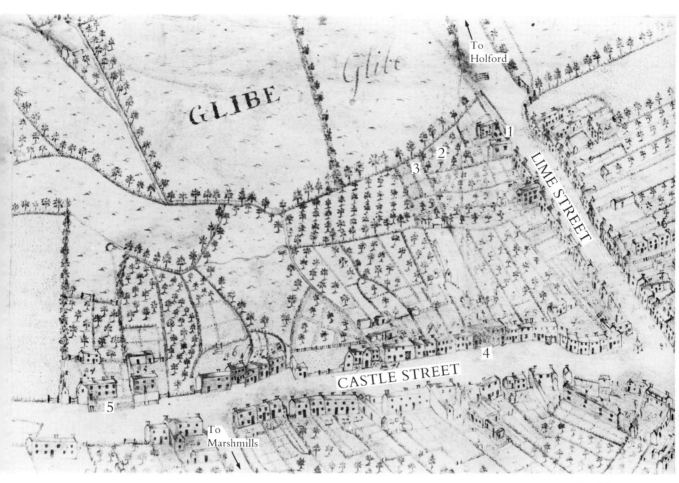

GLIBE

Glibe

To
Holford

LIME STREET

1

2

3

CASTLE STREET

4

5

To
Marshmills

Detail from a late
eighteenth-century
map of Nether
Stowey showing: 1.
Coleridge's cottage;
2. Coleridge's
orchard; 3. Tom
Poole's garden and
the lime-tree bower;
4. Tom Poole's
house; 5. Castle Hill
House, the home of
John Cruikshank

parlour' at the front of the building was soon to become for Coleridge a place in which he felt more at home than in his own tiny cottage, and it was there that he and Poole were later to spend long sociable hours with the Wordsworths, Charles Lamb, Hazlitt and others. A room which served Coleridge in a different way stood at the back of the house on the first floor: this was Tom Poole's vaulted bookroom, created by him early in 1795 and filled with a wide-ranging library which helped to reconcile Coleridge to the loss of his frequent visits to the City Library in Bristol. A flight of external stairs allowed him easy access to the bookroom, and there he must often have been found when the 'noise of Women & children', which made study impossible, had driven him once again from Lime Street: it is probable that most of the poems associated with the cottage were at least partly written in the bookroom.[9]

For both Coleridge and Sara there was the company not only of Tom Poole

Tom Poole's
bookroom

and his much-loved mother, but of new friends as well. John Cruikshank at Castle Hill House and his 'very amiable' wife, Anna, were chief among them, and for Coleridge, at least, there were also a number of admiring and musical young women with whom his puns, conundrums, and attempts at dancing made him 'an immense favorite'. Only in the months ahead did Coleridge and Sara begin to realize how much they had also aroused the hostility and suspicion of inward-looking Stowey, and Coleridge's final verdict on his village neighbours would be a gloomy one. Writing to Poole in April 1799, when the Cruikshanks had gone, he remarked that 'excepting yourself & Mother there is no human being attached to us & few who do not dislike us'.[10]

It was Sara who chiefly bore the social realities of Stowey, the inadequacies of the cottage, and the burdens of parenthood. For Coleridge there was always the immediate possibility of escape, either to the bookroom near at hand, or to the more distant hills. His exploration of the landscape began nearly at once. 'My walks . . . were almost daily on the top of Quantock, and among its sloping coombs,' he recalled in the *Biographia*. 'With my pencil and memorandum book in my hand, I was *making studies*, as the artists call them, and often moulding my thoughts into verse, with the objects and imagery immediately before my senses.' Bewildering doubts and dissatisfied creativity had led him to the hills in search of a poetic subject 'that should give equal room and freedom for description, incident, and impassioned reflections on men, nature, and society'. That capacious subject he considered himself to have found in the stream which rises at the spring called Lady's Fountain, and flows through Holford Combe and Holford Glen on its short journey to the sea at Kilve. 'The Brook', as the intended poem was to be called, would trace the fictionalized stream from its origins 'among the yellow-red moss and conical glass-shaped tufts of bent' to the first lonely cottage, and ultimately to 'the market-town, the manufactories, and the seaport'. He was to follow the course of the stream many times, latterly in the company of William and Dorothy Wordsworth. But the poem progressed farther in the mind than on paper, and all that survives of it are some verse fragments describing the distant wail of swallows and seagulls, water dripping one Sunday from the miller's wheel (perhaps at Kilve), the snow blown curling from a wood 'like pillars of cottage smoke', and a wild Quantock pony racing in the wind.[11]

Other projects made more rapid progress that new year. At the end of January an invitation from Richard Brinsley Sheridan to write a tragedy for Drury Lane left Coleridge 'gratified and somewhat elated', and vowing that whatever time he could spare from reviewing he would now devote to play-writing. He embarked soon after on his long verse-tragedy *Osorio*, a story 'romantic & wild & somewhat terrible', which he set in Spain at the time of the Inquisition, but which was to draw, at least to a small extent, on his Quantock and Exmoor wanderings

The brook in
Holford Combe

of the next few months. A new edition of his poems was also in prospect from Joseph Cottle, augmented, when it appeared in October, by substantial contributions from Charles Lamb and Charles Lloyd, and by a generous poem of dedication addressed with a childlike longing for acceptance to Coleridge's brother George, his 'earliest Friend'. (George, sad to record, 'was displeased and thought his character endangered by the Dedication'.)[12]

Only as the calls upon him grew more insistent did Coleridge's mood darken. By mid-March he was far behind with the reviewing on which he now chiefly depended for a living, Cottle was becoming 'clamorous' about preparations for the new edition of poems, and *Osorio* was a commitment which seemed likely to reach for months into the future. Circumstances at Lime Street did nothing to improve his state of mind. Although there is no hint in his letters from the Stowey period of differences with Sara, it is likely that the subtle process of estrangement was already under way. His twin devotions to Quantock solitude and the company of Tom Poole brought not only physical separation from the Lime Street cottage, but a widening emotional distance from his forthright, practical, and hard-pressed wife: it would not be long before the autumn happiness of their Clevedon days was a distant memory. Difficulties of a more acute kind began with the arrival of Charles Lloyd on 22 February. Coleridge had

One of the bedrooms in the Lime Street cottage

73

discovered during the final weeks at Bristol that the devoted but unstable Lloyd was subject to attacks of mania and was a sufferer from epilepsy. During March, established as a lodger in one of the upstairs bedrooms, his illness returned. 'He has been seized with his fits three times in the space of seven days,' Coleridge wrote to Joseph Cottle on 15 March; 'and just as I was in bed, last night, I was called up again – and from 12 o clock at night to *five* this morning he remained in one *continued* state of *agoniz'd Delirium*.'[13]

By the end of the month Lloyd had retreated to Erasmus Darwin's sanatorium in Lichfield, and Coleridge to Bristol, on the first of two short visits. During the first visit he was in such low spirits he could not bring himself to meet even the faithful Cottle; during the second, in early April, optimism and humour had sufficiently returned for him to relish a meeting with one especially talkative woman on his homeward walk. She asked if he knew a 'vile jacobin villain' who had led astray a young man from her parish called Burnett. The villain in question was a certain Coleridge, upon whom she proceeded to heap 'every name of abuse that the parish of Billingsgate could supply'. The man himself, walking mildly at her side, had by some inevitable process succeeded in charming his travelling companion, and 'had not courage enough to undeceive her'.[14]

April brought another and more significant meeting to raise Coleridge from 'calm hopelessness' and financial worry. Early in the month William Wordsworth, returning from Bristol to the home he was sharing near Crewkerne with his sister Dorothy, made a detour into West Somerset to visit Coleridge. At their first meetings in Bristol during the autumn of 1795 each had at once recognized in the other a man of extraordinary abilities. It seems clear that they had corresponded during 1796, and by the time they met again at Stowey they were well acquainted with each other's work. Now came the opportunity for long discussions in Tom Poole's parlour, and no doubt for readings from *Osorio* and from *The Borderers*, Wordsworth's own, equally unsuccessful, verse tragedy. Coleridge was overwhelmed, as he made plain in a letter to Joseph Cottle: 'T. Poole's opinion of Wordsworth is – that he is the greatest Man, he ever knew – I coincide.'[15]

His imaginative pulse quickened almost at once, and in the second week of May he was able to report that no fewer than 1,500 lines of *Osorio* had been completed. His mood also soared. When the sub-librarian of the Bristol City Library wrote on the subject of overdue books, Coleridge managed a *tour de force* of consternation in reply (the recipient was not amused). In these weeks he was also carrying his tireless eloquence to local Unitarian chapels. Unitarianism, a tolerant and loosely-defined system of belief, had attracted Coleridge since his Cambridge years. Of all varieties of the Christian faith, it seemed best able to accommodate his persistent search for a means to link the truths of philosophy

Interior of Mary Street Unitarian Chapel, Taunton. The Bible is the same that Coleridge used on his many preaching visits to the chapel

Lithograph of the Cistercian abbey at Forde, Dorset, 1875

and religion, and his almost pantheistic sense of the 'Absolute Unity' shared by God and his creation. He had asked John Prior Estlin for letters of introduction to the Unitarian ministers at Bridgwater and Taunton, and became a regular preacher in both towns for as long as he remained at Stowey. On Sunday 4 June 1797 he preached for Mr Howel at the Dampiet Street Chapel in Bridgwater, taking as his Coleridgean theme 'the contemptibleness & evil of lukewarmness'. Immediately afterwards, he set off on a journey into Dorset, determined to repay Wordsworth's visit of two months earlier. He breakfasted at Taunton with Joshua Toulmin, the town's kindly and distinguished Unitarian minister, then continued west through Neroche Forest towards Horton Cross and Chard. Lukewarmness was far from his prevailing mood as he strode onwards.[16]

☆

The landscape south-east of Chard is remote and beautiful. Broad, well-wooded valleys mark its character. Streams flow abundantly into the little River Axe, and close to the meeting-point of three counties a secluded no man's land contains the

John Pretor Pinney
(1740–1818), the
owner of Racedown
Lodge

exquisite Forde Abbey, its Cistercian isolation still largely undisturbed. Marshwood Vale lies farther south, expansive and lovely, and extends from Hardy's 'little Pilsdon Crest' to a horizon which is the sea. It was in a fold of high ground on the northern borders of the vale that William Wordsworth and his sister Dorothy had recently taken up residence in a red-brick mansion called Racedown Lodge, a house combining Georgian elegance and merchant stolidity, and quite likely to be, as tradition asserts, the original of Sir Walter Elliot's Kellynch Hall in Jane Austen's *Persuasion*.[17]

Despite the stateliness of their domestic setting, Wordsworth and his sister were hardly more financially secure at Racedown than the household at Lime Street, and owed the possibility of living there to the brothers John and Azariah Pinney. The Pinneys had become devoted admirers of William Wordsworth after meeting him in London during 1795, and had soon persuaded their father, John Pretor Pinney, that the little-used family mansion in Dorset should become Wordsworth's temporary home. The elder Pinney, owner of the largest sugar plantations in Nevis, would certainly have been less pliable had he realized that his sons were allowing the new tenants to have Racedown rent-free; but in the event he quickly warmed to the young poet, and welcomed him as a guest to the family's town house in Bristol during the autumn of 1795, the period which first brought Wordsworth into contact with both Coleridge and Southey.[18]

William and Dorothy Wordsworth arrived at Racedown Lodge one midnight near the end of September 1795, and were to remain tenants there for almost two years. For both of them a period of deep contentment had begun. 'I think Racedown is the place dearest to my recollections upon the whole surface of the island,' Dorothy later wrote. 'It was the first home I had.' The extent of their happiness as they read and wrote, and walked the Dorset lanes, was in proportion to the unsettled times they had often known until then. The death of their mother, Ann Wordsworth, in 1778, when William was seven and Dorothy six, had cast a long shadow over their early lives, and had left them and their three brothers effectively orphaned. Their father, John Wordsworth, a law-agent in Cockermouth, sent Dorothy to be brought up in Halifax by a relative, and before long had enrolled William in a boarding-school at Hawkshead. Dorothy did not see her brother again for nine years, and never once returned to the family home in Cockermouth before the death of her father in 1783. She never ceased to regret that her own family had been scattered while she was still so young, and when, in 1787, the five Wordsworth children were briefly reunited, they returned constantly to a single theme. 'We always finish our conversations', Dorothy wrote, '. . . with wishing we had a father and a home.'[19]

In the summer of 1789, after Wordsworth had become an undergraduate at St John's College, Cambridge, a long visit to Dorothy at their uncle's house in Norfolk confirmed between brother and sister a profound emotional sympathy which remained with them through life, and made them certain that, one day, they wished to share a home. The opportunity to do so did not arise until Racedown was offered to them six years later, by which time Wordsworth could contemplate a life whose course, since his Norfolk visit, had done much to shape his political and poetic character, and had left him with more than a little to repent. He walked heroic distances through France, Switzerland, and Germany in the summer vacation of 1790, discovering for himself the realities of France in the throes of revolution, and the sublimities of the Alps. The following summer was devoted to a walking tour in North Wales, during which he climbed Snowdon to watch the sun rise – an experience, like his crossing of the Alps, destined to inspire some of the most celebrated poetry in *The Prelude*. He was in France again at the end of 1791, and in the new year at Orléans evidently formed the relationship with Annette Vallon which resulted that December in the birth of their illegitimate daughter Caroline. Caroline was only a few days old when Wordsworth left for home, and during 1793, marooned in England without an income or particular hopes of finding one, he learned helplessly of the rise of the Terror in France following the overthrow of the Girondins in June that year.

His relations gave him up, deploring his French expedition and the revolutionary sympathies it so clearly implied, and despairing that he would ever take the opportunities available to him for making a career in the Church or the law. He wrote the poetry of social conscience in the remarkable *Salisbury Plain*, and imbibed the radicalism of friends and acquaintances in London; but the vagabond

Silhouette of
Dorothy
Wordsworth (1771–
1855). This is the
only known likeness
of Dorothy as a
young woman

existence to which he was increasingly reduced lacked in every sense a clear
direction. Dorothy alone remained a still centre, and when in January 1795
Wordsworth was left £900 in the will of Raisley Calvert, a young friend and
admirer who had died of tuberculosis, there seemed nothing further to prevent
them from realizing their hopes of a life together.

☆

79

Racedown Lodge from the garden

The parlour at
Racedown Lodge

By the time Wordsworth finally set out from Bristol to Racedown in the autumn
of 1795, he had, in the words of *The Prelude*, 'Yielded up moral questions in
despair'. The dawn of hope signalled by the French Revolution had ended as
murderous confusion, and radicalism in England was increasingly under attack
from both repressive government and popular opinion. Just as Coleridge in 1796
abandoned political life in dismay, so Wordsworth now turned from politics in
search of another version of his friend's 'deep Sabbath of meek self-content'. It
was Dorothy who provided the watchful, loving companionship which, as he
famously acknowledged in Book X of *The Prelude*, helped a new sense of self to
be resolved from his doubts and confusions:

> . . . then it was
> That the belovèd Woman in whose sight
> Those days were pass'd, now speaking in a voice
> Of sudden admonition, like a brook
> That does but cross a lonely road, and now
> Seen, heard and felt, and caught at every turn,
> Companion never lost through many a league,
> Maintain'd for me a saving intercourse

Hinton House,
Hinton St Georg
the seat of Earl
Poulett, 1791

> With my true self . . .
> She, in the midst of all, preserv'd me still
> A Poet, made me seek beneath that name
> My office upon earth, and nowhere else.

It was a tribute for which the events of the next three years provided ample justification.[20]

The Wordsworths were not alone at Racedown, despite the remoteness of its setting. Joseph Gill, John Pinney's hard-drinking cousin, lived near by as caretaker; Peggy Marsh, described by Dorothy as 'one of the nicest girls I ever saw', arrived after a month to help in running the enormous house; and from the beginning Wordsworth and Dorothy were preoccupied with caring for a child not yet three years old called Basil Montagu. Basil's widowed father, a natural son of the Earl of Sandwich, formed part of Wordsworth's circle of London friends, and the proposal that Wordsworth and Dorothy should become responsible for the child was from the beginning an important part of their plans for life at Racedown. 'He is my perpetual pleasure,' Dorothy wrote in March 1796. 'He is quite metamorphosed from a shivering half starved plant, to a lusty, blooming fearless boy.' Recalling, no doubt, the sad disruptions of her own early life, she declared that 'our grand study has been to make him *happy*', and added that under their Rousseau-inspired regime, in which Basil was taught nothing 'but what he learns from the evidence of his senses', he had become 'certainly the most contented child I ever saw; the least disposed to be fretful.'[21]

His father, also called Basil, visited briefly in March 1797; John and Azariah Pinney stayed on a number of occasions, and at greater length. But the ordinary distractions of Racedown life were sought among books, in a vegetable garden soon filled with cabbages, carrots and turnips, and in the hills. Some of these, Dorothy reported approvingly, remained 'in their wild state covered with furze and broom', and reminded her of her native north country. Crewkerne, the nearest post town, was the frequent destination of other walks, and on one occasion Wordsworth and Dorothy continued a few miles further to take in Hinton House, the home of Earl Poulett. They discovered not only the Poulett mansion but a very fine view, perhaps from the Warren House above the park, and were, Dorothy wrote to a friend, 'amply repaid' for their trouble.[22]

Their lives, described by Wordsworth in 1796 as 'utterly barren' of conventional excitements, might have continued undisturbed at Racedown had the choice been entirely theirs. But by the end of May 1797, with the countryside bursting suddenly into beauty after the coldest spring Dorothy could remember, they knew that their unorthodox tenancy was not likely to continue: John Pretor Pinney was already looking for rent-paying tenants. In the event, the ending of their two Dorset years came with dramatic suddenness, and brought not a narrowing of their lives, as they might have feared, but the beginning of a period marked by profound and creative friendship. Occupied in their garden on a June day in 1797, they looked up to see a figure standing in a gateway at the top of the gentle slope one hundred yards from the mansion. A moment later, having leapt the gate, Samuel Taylor Coleridge was bounding down a pathless field towards them.[23]

Chapter Five

'WORDSWORTH & HIS EXQUISITE SISTER'

Coleridge's headlong arrival into the lives of William and Dorothy Wordsworth remained for them all a charged and exhilarating memory. Speaking of the event almost fifty years later, Wordsworth said that both he and his sister retained 'the liveliest possible image' of Coleridge in that moment, and Coleridge himself regarded the warmth with which he was received at Racedown as a standard against which all other greetings could be measured and found to fall short. At first his visit was intended to last only a few days. Very quickly, however, the three young people began to exert over one another the complex mutual attraction which remained characteristic of their relationship, and more than three weeks passed before Coleridge finally set off on the road back to Stowey.[1]

Deepening friendship and shared creativity marked those weeks together. Within hours of his arrival, Coleridge was listening to Wordsworth recite a substantial new poem called 'The Ruined Cottage'; after tea Coleridge replied with two and a half acts of *Osorio*, and in the morning followed the whole of *The Borderers*, Wordsworth's north country tragedy. Coleridge thought *The Borderers* 'absolutely wonderful', and surrounded only by the distractions of friendship and a lovely, unfamiliar countryside, found time at Racedown to make progress with his own play, Wordsworth providing the necessary encouragement as well as some 'strict & almost severe' criticism. By the sixth day at Racedown, Coleridge had reached a settled opinion of his host: 'Wordsworth is a great man,' he wrote to John Prior Estlin in Bristol, a compliment which Wordsworth, half a lifetime later, repaid in subtly different terms when he described Coleridge as 'the most *wonderful* man I ever knew'.[2]

Dorothy's acute and sympathetic judgement that Racedown summer led her to a similar conclusion almost at once. 'You had a great loss in not seeing Coleridge,' she wrote to a friend at the end of June. 'He is a wonderful man.' In a passage of intense and fascinated observation, she then continued:

His conversation teems with soul, mind, and spirit. Then he is so benevolent, so good tempered and cheerful, and, like William, interests himself so much about every little trifle. At first I thought him very plain, that is, for about three

gateway above
edown Lodge

Samuel Taylor
Coleridge in 1795
Portrait by Peter
Vandyke

minutes: he is pale and thin, has a wide mouth, thick lips, and not very good teeth, longish loose-growing half-curling rough black hair. But if you hear him speak for five minutes you think no more of them. His eye is large and full, not dark but grey; such an eye as would receive from a heavy soul the dullest expression; but it speaks every emotion of his animated mind; it has more of the 'poet's eye in a fine frenzy rolling' than I ever witnessed. He has fine dark eyebrows, and an overhanging forehead.[3]

Coleridge's opinion of Dorothy was soon to be recorded by him in words no less intense, and by the time he parted from the Wordsworths on 28 June, they were all determined that their separation from one another should be as brief as possible.

☆

To the pleasures of new friendship, Coleridge, on his return to Stowey, added the prospect of meeting again the loyal and longstanding friend of his youth, Charles Lamb. Lamb had finally yielded to an invitation from Coleridge to travel west, and wrote at the end of June to say that he hoped to arrive at Stowey the following week. Coleridge, his thoughts still at Racedown, immediately saw the opportunity for bringing all his friends together at Stowey, and on 29 June wrote to Joseph Cottle to suggest – unsuccessfully – that he should take the next coach to Bridgwater: 'T. Poole would fetch you in a one horse Chair.' More important, he set about gathering the Wordsworths into the Quantock fold, hastening a visit which must in any case have been intended for the near future. Wordsworth arrived almost at once, and by 2 July Dorothy had also reached Lime Street, after being driven up from Dorset by Coleridge himself 'over forty miles of execrable road'.[4]

Charles Lamb (1775–1834) in 1798. After a pencil and chalk drawing by Robert Hancock

The difficulty of finding room for his guests in so small a house was farthest from Coleridge's mind. He was filled with a passionate delight in the company of his friends, of Dorothy especially, and joyfully announced in a letter to Joseph Cottle the news that 'Wordsworth & his exquisite Sister' had arrived:

She is a woman indeed! – in mind, I mean, & heart – for her person is such, that if you expected to see a pretty woman, you would think her ordinary – if you expected to find an ordinary woman, you would think her pretty! – But her manners are simple, ardent, impressive . . . Her information various – her eye watchful in minutest observation of nature – and her taste a perfect electro-meter – it bends, protrudes, and draws in, at subtlest beauties & most recondite faults.[5]

To Sara, more hard-pressed than ever at Lime Street, the intellectual and emotional sympathy binding Coleridge and Dorothy must have been both apparent and distressing, even if Dorothy, in De Quincey's words, was a woman possessing 'no personal charms': on only the second day of the visit Coleridge and Dorothy were occupied together correcting his poems for the new edition while Sara was left to carry the domestic burdens of the teeming cottage. One minor incident, soon after the Wordsworths arrived, seemed by accident to express the complex emotions which underlay those high-spirited weeks in the summer of 1797. Sara upset a skillet of boiling milk on her husband's foot, and left him so lame that he was prevented for days from joining his friends on their lengthening excursions into the Quantock countryside. While the Wordsworths began to explore a landscape which seemed, in Dorothy's opinion, to contain everything she could want, Coleridge remained very unwillingly at home.[6]

It was probably at his suggestion that the Wordsworths walked one evening to Holford, a small village three miles west from Stowey on the road to Putsham and Kilve. There, in a wooded dell called Holford Glen, close to the village church, they found an almost inaccessible waterfall which interrupted the Holford brook on its journey to the sea, and which, for them as for Coleridge, quickly became almost a voice of nature, an abiding, animated presence at the heart of their Quantock lives. They 'pryed into the recesses' of the brook which flowed from the waterfall, then followed a lonely road next to the Glen through a woodland of beeches, oaks, and holly, where sheep from the Quantocks and fallow deer moved in the evening light. Whether knowingly or not, the Wordsworths had entered the deer park surrounding a large unoccupied mansion called Alfoxden, and reached the house itself before deciding to turn back.[7]

The park at Alfoxden had belonged to the St Albyn family since the close of the fifteenth century. But their Queen Anne mansion, four-square and elegant, had seldom been occupied since the Revd Lancelot St Albyn, last in the male line, had been carried to his grave at Stringston in 1791. His widow, Anna-Maria St Albyn, did not choose to live in so isolated a place, and her great nephew, heir to

the estate, was still a child. Those were details unknown to the Wordsworths when they first saw the house, standing alone on its hillside site between the Quantocks and the sea. They knew only, as they retraced their steps through the deep woodland of the park, that they could no longer be content at Racedown, even had it been possible for them to remain there. 'Coleridge's society' had become indispensable, and by the time they made their way back into Lime Street their minds were already filled with 'dreams of happiness', to be lived out, they hoped, in some cottage not far away.[8]

Charles Lamb reached Stowey on about 7 July, and although, as a London man, he was apt to be contemptuous of mere countryside, he joined the Wordsworths uncomplainingly on their expeditions. Coleridge, still lame, chafed at his own confinement, especially when his friends set off one evening towards the hills, leaving him useless and lonely in Tom Poole's garden arbour. Poetry was the result. While Coleridge waited for the sun to set behind Dowsborough

Watercolour of Alfoxden from the south. This is the earliest known picture of the house, and shows it in the first half of the nineteenth century before the ground level at the front of the building was raised

Overleaf: Detail from Day and Masters' map of Somerset, 1782

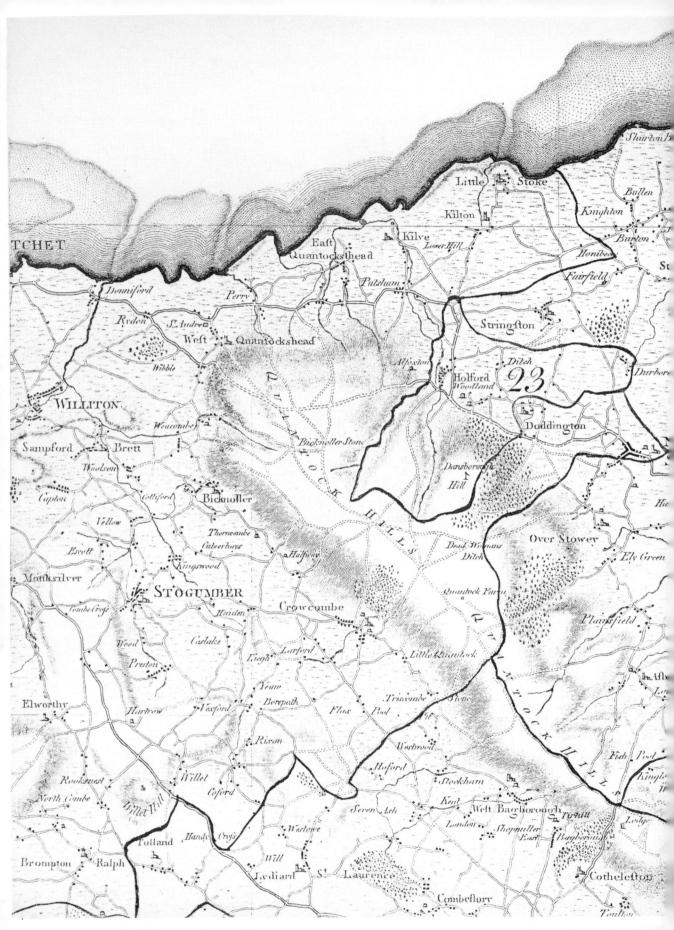

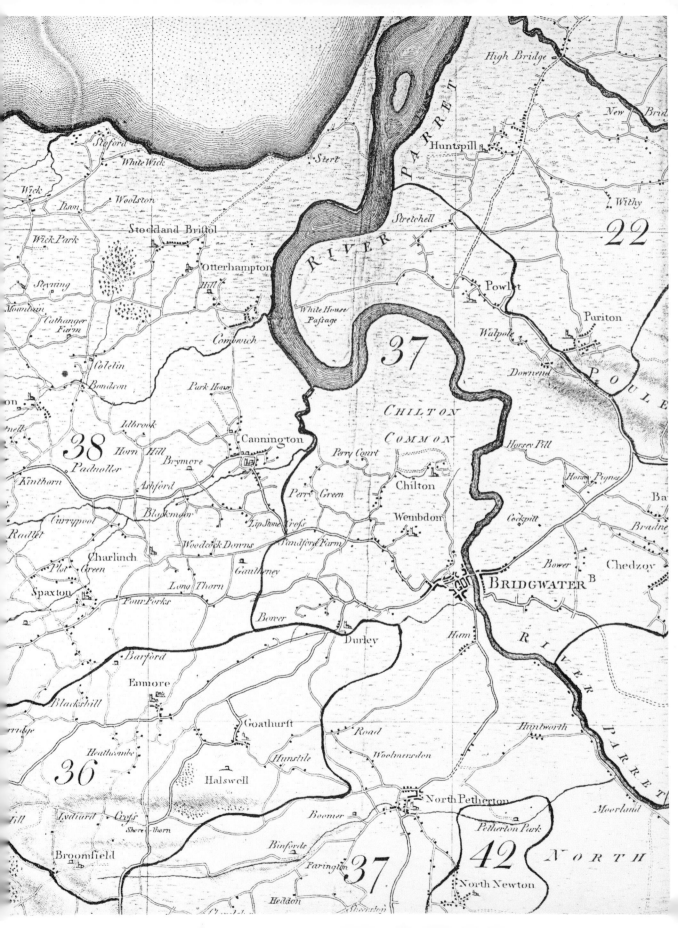

and Higher Hare Knap, he wrote the first fluent draft of a poem reworked soon afterwards as 'This Lime-Tree Bower My Prison'. The poem, addressed in its final form to Charles Lamb, followed his friends in imagination as they walked first 'along the hill-top edge', then descended to the waterfall in the 'roaring dell' at Holford, and climbed at last high into the Quantocks, from where they looked out upon 'the many-steepled tract magnificent' of the coastal plain. The poem is Coleridge's tribute of friendship to his 'gentle-hearted Charles' – Lamb complained later that he would have preferred 'drunken-dog' to 'gentle-hearted' – but it is a tribute equally to the quickening power of the natural beauty which the poem so memorably evokes.[9]

The distinctive moods of the rich and various landscapes which crowded near to Stowey were becoming for Coleridge almost a reflex of his own moods and thoughts – the broad uplands of the Quantock Hills a counterpoint to the speculative power of a mind 'habituated *to the vast*', the lowland villages an expression for him of the loving companionship of friends and family, the hidden dell, where the voice of nature sounded in the waterfall, a retreat by turns comforting and mysterious to serve his recurrent longing for escape.

As he gathered up his papers in the lime-tree bower, and returned through his orchard to the cottage, the most poetically creative year of his life was just beginning.

The tentative search by the Wordsworths for a Somerset home brought the unexpected discovery, probably made by Tom Poole, that Alfoxden was both empty and available. John Bartholomew of Putsham, evidently tenant of the Alfoxden home farm, was persuaded that the Wordsworths should take the house for a year, at a rent of only £23, and on 14 July 1797 an agreement was hastily drawn up in Poole's 'villainous hand-scrawl' and signed by Bartholomew and Wordsworth. Old Mrs St Albyn was not consulted.[10]

The new tenants moved into the house at once, and the arrival soon afterwards of their servant Peggy Marsh and young Basil Montagu was final confirmation that the Racedown years were at an end. Coleridge was in a state of profound happiness and lingering disbelief when he wrote to Robert Southey of the 'combination of curious circumstances' which had brought the Wordsworths to Alfoxden. The mansion was, he said, 'elegantly & completely *furnished* – with 9 *lodging rooms*, three parlours & a Hall – in a most beautiful & romantic situation by the sea side'. Nor did Dorothy quickly shake off a sense of their improbable good fortune. She began a letter a month after their arrival with the words, 'Here we are in a large mansion, in a large park, with seventy head of deer around us', before going on to describe a house which contained 'furniture enough for a dozen families like ours'.[11]

Alfoxden had been built by the St Albyns early in the eighteenth century close

The entrance hall a Alfoxden, photographed duri the 1930s

to the centre of their ancient park. It faced south towards a steep slope which gave way, beyond a thick and irregular scattering of trees, to the furze and bracken of the Quantock high ground. Behind the house fields and woodland dropped gently away towards the sea coast at Lilstock, Kilve and East Quantoxhead, and it was this view which Dorothy and her brother could see from the tall sash-windows of their favourite parlour. Dorothy was overwhelmed by the beauty which surrounded them:

> Wherever we turn we have woods, smooth downs, and valleys with small brooks running down them through green meadows . . . The hills that cradle these valleys are either covered with fern and bilberries, or oak woods, which are cut for charcoal . . . Walks extend for miles over the hill-tops; the great beauty of which is their wild simplicity: they are perfectly smooth, without rocks.[12]

A housewarming was impulsively decided on to mark the arrival of the new Alfoxden tenants, and on about 17 July Coleridge, seeking 'change of air', arrived from Stowey in anticipation of the event. Though Charles Lamb had by now returned to London – envying his forgotten greatcoat for 'lingering so cunningly behind' at Lime Street – the sudden appearance of John Thelwall was more than compensation. 'Citizen' John, 'a little Stout Man with dark cropt Hair', carried with him a dangerous reputation as an atheist, a mob orator and a Jacobin, and in 1794 had spent several months in the Tower of London before being tried and acquitted on a charge of high treason.[13] His relationship with Coleridge had hitherto depended entirely on their animated and frequently argumentative correspondence. Now, at first meeting, they laid the foundations of a more substantial friendship in the groves of Alfoxden, two disillusioned radicals who had turned their backs on active politics. 'John Thelwall is a very warm hearted honest man,' Coleridge wrote to Josiah Wade, 'and disagreeing, as we do, on almost every point of religion, of morals, of politics, and of philosophy; we like each other uncommonly well.' He was taken on the indispensable visit to Holford Glen, and it was there, seated by the side of the brook, that the brief exchange took place which Coleridge was still repeating in his old age: 'Citizen John,' Coleridge remarked, 'this is a fine place to talk treason in!' To which Thelwall replied, 'Nay! Citizen Samuel! It is rather a place to make a man forget that there is any necessity for treason!'[14]

The housewarming dinner was arranged for Sunday 23 July 1797, and on the day before, Coleridge scribbled a hasty, high-spirited note to Tom Poole asking for a promised fore quarter of lamb to be sent over to 'the Foxes' in the morning. 'I pray you,' he added, 'come over if possible by eleven o'clock that we may have Wordsworths Tragedy read under the Trees.' Fourteen people sat down to dinner at the house, a local man, Thomas Jones, being employed to wait on them at table. Jones was struck especially by Citizen Thelwall, who, wearing the white

Coleridge's letter 22 July 1797 to T[..] Poole, asking that fore quarter of Lamb' be sent ov[..] for the Alfoxden housewarming

94

My dear Poole

We have taken a fore quarter of lamb from your mother — which you will be so kind, according to your word, or (as the wit said to a minister of state) notwithstanding your promise, to send over to the Foxes to morrow morning by a boy —

I pray you, come over if possible by eleven o'clock that we may have Wordsworths Tragedy read under the Trees — S. T. Coleridge

hat of the radical, got up after dinner and 'talked so loud and was in such a Passion that Jones was frightened'. Other guests probably included Stowey friends such as John and Anna Cruikshank. But Tom Poole's cousins at Marshmills were not invited, and would in any case have been horrified to find themselves among this conclave of radicals. On the very day of the dinner Charlotte Poole was writing in her journal: 'We are shocked to hear that Mr. Thelwall has spent some time at Stowey this week with Mr. Coleridge, and consequently with Tom Poole. Alfoxton house is taken by one of the fraternity . . . To what are we coming?'[15]

Charlotte Poole was not alone in feeling suspicious and alarmed. Although the people of Stowey had by degrees reconciled themselves to the presence of Coleridge, who lived in their midst with his wife and child, Wordsworth's arrival at remote Alfoxden, with a young woman said to be his sister, provided much greater scope for speculation. 'The wiseacres of the village', so Joseph Cottle heard from Coleridge, 'had . . . made Mr. W. the subject of their serious conversation' and concluded that a man so given to wandering the hills at late hours 'like a partridge', and looking strangely at the moon, must either be a conjuror, a smuggler, or worst of all 'a desperd French jacobin' who was spying out the ground for a French invasion. It was the last view which the locals were readiest to believe. As recently as January that year, the people of North Devon had been 'greatly alarmed' by three French frigates and a lugger seen making their way up the Bristol Channel off Ilfracombe. This optimistic French sortie, intended to achieve the burning of Bristol, had ended disastrously at Fishguard, but both the West Country and the government remained fearful.[16]

Gossip which might have remained merely an irritation led by accident to altogether more dangerous consequences.[17] From Thomas Jones, who had been so frightened by Thelwall's oratory, stories concerning the 'emigrant family' at Alfoxden passed first to Charles Mogg – a former servant at the house – and then to a cook in the household of Dr Daniel Lysons of Bath. When the stories reached Lysons himself, he wrote at once to the Duke of Portland, the home secretary, alerting him to the 'very suspicious business' taking place at Alfoxden, and on 11 August a government spy called James Walsh was dispatched to investigate. Walsh went first to Hungerford in search of Charles Mogg – 'by no means the most intelligent Man in the World' – and from him received a detailed account of his conversations with Thomas Jones and other villagers at Holford. What appeared to be the most damaging evidence had been provided by an old man called Christopher Tricky, who lived in a hovel near the dog pound at Alfoxden park gate:

Christopher Trickie and his Wife . . . told Mogg that the French people had taken the plan of their House, and that They had also taken the plan of all the

A cottage on Holford Common. Watercolour by W.A. Rixon, 1899. When Wordsworth revisited Holford in 1841, Christopher Tricky's hovel on the common had already disappeared

places round that part of the Country, that a Brook runs in the front of Trickie's House and the French people inquired of Trickie wether the Brook was Navigable to the Sea, and upon being informed by Trickie that It was not, they were afterwards seen examining the Brook quite down to the Sea.

Wordsworth probably never knew how his walks with Dorothy and Coleridge had been misrepresented by the garrulous old man, and would have been sorry to discover the truth. Christopher Tricky, formerly a huntsman to the St Albyn family, was the inspiration for Wordsworth's poem 'Simon Lee, the Old Huntsman', in which Tricky's vigorous youth and poverty-stricken old age stand in sad contrast. He was, perhaps, less than worthy of his literary immortality: in 1800 the vicar of Over Stowey, having been cheated in a deal over some turf, called him 'as rascally faced fellow as ever I met with'.[18]

Walsh reached the Globe Inn at Stowey on 15 August 1797 with instructions to give a 'precise account' of anything he discovered, and to seek necessary help from Sir Philip Hales, a magistrate living at Brymore in Cannington. Walsh's investigations made more rapid progress than he can have expected. At the bar of the Globe Inn talk between the landlord and a Mr Woodhouse of Stowey turned very quickly to the subject of 'those Rascalls from Alfoxden' and of John Thelwall, who had left for Bristol two weeks earlier. 'I . . . asked if they meant the famous Thelwall,' Walsh reported. 'They said yes. That he had been down some time, and that there were a Nest of them at Alfoxden House who were

The former Globe
Inn, Nether Stow
where James Wals
the government s
stayed in 1795

protected by a Mr Poole a Tanner of this Town.' Walsh was assured that the
people concerned were not French – though they were as bad – and he quickly
concluded that he was dealing with no more than 'a mischiefuous gang of
disaffected Englishmen'. There followed three weeks during which, in Coleridge's comical retelling of events, Walsh displayed 'truly Indian perseverance' in
tracking the poets on their daily excursions into the hills and down to the beach at
Kilve. At first, so Coleridge improbably claimed, Walsh thought he had been
found out: 'for he heard me talk of one *Spy Nozy*, which he was inclined to
interpret of himself, and of a remarkable feature belonging to him'. The pun on
Spinoza was too good for Coleridge to resist, and the remarkable nose he
attributed to Walsh may well have been borrowed from his memories of the
innkeeper at the Castle of Comfort, on the road from Stowey to Holford: his
nose, which was locally famous, was said to be as big as a fist and 'well warted'.[19]

The end of the spy story reached Coleridge from the innkeeper of the Globe,
who had been ordered to Brymore by Sir Philip Hales ('Sir Dogberry' as
Coleridge called him) to give evidence in person. The innkeeper, in Coleridge's
version of events, could remember nothing remotely suspicious in the activities
either of Coleridge or the 'strange gentleman' from Alfoxden, though he did
recall the amazement of some local farmers when, at a great dinner party,
Coleridge and the vicar of Stowey had talked 'real Hebrew Greek at each other

Sir Philip Hales, Bt.
(d. 1824), in a
caricature by John
Chubb of
Bridgwater

for an hour together'. Sir Philip angrily pressed the innkeeper to say whatever he knew of Coleridge, and was at last told the innocent truth:

'Why, folks do say, your honor! as how that he is a *Poet*, and that he is going to put Quantock and all about here in print; and as they be so much together, I suppose that the strange gentleman has some *consarn* in the business.'[20]

Walsh departed, and although Coleridge later refused to see the 'Spy Nozy' incident as other than ridiculous, the government's unwanted attentions had marked a time of real danger, as John Thelwall, from bitter recent experience, could have warned. Local rumour, for its part, had blackened the reputation of both poets beyond recovery, and by late August Coleridge realized that Thelwall's own hopes of settling near Stowey were not only unrealistic but dangerous. Coleridge wrote sadly to tell him so:

Very great odium T. Poole incurred by bringing *me* here . . . when Words-worth came & he likewise by T. Poole's agency settled here – You cannot conceive the tumult, calumnies, & apparatus of threatened persecutions which this event has occasioned round about us. If *you* too should come, I am afraid, that even riots & dangerous riots might be the consequence.[21]

A romanticized vie
of Culbone Combe
1803

Mrs St Albyn had before long heard the unpleasant rumours concerning the new tenants at Alfoxden, and ordered, in spite of Tom Poole's intercession, that on no account should they remain at the mansion beyond the following midsummer. As the autumn of 1797 approached time was already running out.

At the end of August 1797 Coleridge was in low spirits and unwell, worn down by the 'Malignity of the Aristocrats', who had brought the spy to Stowey, by the need to disappoint John Thelwall's hopes of a Somerset home, and by poverty. Charles Lloyd had returned to Lime Street by September, but his presence was now more clearly a burden than a pleasure, and his mental instability was soon to result in what Coleridge bitterly recollected as a 'mad quarrel' and in vindictive ingratitude. On 14 October Coleridge wrote abstractedly to John Thelwall that, 'I should much wish, like the Indian Vishna, to float about along an infinite ocean cradled in the flower of the Lotos, & wake once in a million years for a few minutes – just to know that I was going to sleep a million years more.' This comforting vision, perhaps opium-inspired, was far removed from the reality surrounding him at Stowey. 'I have neither money or influence,' he hold Thelwall, '& I suppose, that at last I must become a Unitarian minister as a less evil than starvation – for I get nothing by literature.'[22]

His despondent letter to Thelwall was written immediately following an absence of 'a day or two', during which, it seems likely, he walked westward into the Exmoor fringes above Porlock, the home territory of his maternal ancestors, and in a lonely farmhouse near Culbone Church sought the isolation he needed to complete *Osorio*. The wild and beautiful landscape around Culbone rises with dramatic suddenness from the Bristol Channel coast near Porlock Weir. Within a mile of the sea the bracken-covered hills of Exmoor, deeply intersected by wooded combes, reach heights of over 1,000 feet, and only on the lower slopes do farmers derive a living from the inhospitable soil. It was a landscape which Coleridge probably knew well by the time of his autumn visit, and to whose

Culbone Church. The truncated spire, echoing the spire at Porlock, was added during the nineteenth century

Ash Farm, Porlock, usually identified as the farm where 'Kubla Khan' was written

spectacular beauty he was to introduce the Wordsworths before the year ended. He followed a difficult zigzag path from Porlock Weir to Culbone, climbing through woodland which abounded in 'wild deer, foxes, badgers, and martin cats'; whortleberries grew in plenty beneath the canopy of trees, and as the ascent progressed, the distant sound of waves breaking on the shore below and glimpses of the Channel and the Welsh mountains were sufficient to fill one eighteenth-century traveller with mingled 'pleasure and astonishment'.[23]

At 450 feet the church was reached, standing utterly secluded in the deep folds of Culbone Combe. Reputedly the smallest of England's parish churches, it may have developed from an anchorite's cell in the eleventh or twelfth century, and since that time had drawn many pilgrims to its almost inaccessible woodland site. James Hadley, writing his will in 1532, remembered the church as one of Somerset's 'holy places', and by the late eighteenth century it had become the frequent destination of topographical writers who came searching for the romantically sublime. Coleridge had little sympathy with their overheated prose, and his own response to this charged and mysterious place probably had more in common with that of a later visitor, Samuel Palmer, who in the nineteenth century saw Culbone through visionary eyes.[24]

Coleridge said in later life that the farmhouse to which he now retreated was called Brimstone (no doubt a Coleridgean attempt at Broomstreet, which stood two miles west of the combe). His more contemporary recollection, however, placed the farmhouse 'a quarter of a mile from Culbone Church', a description which has almost always been said to identify Ash Farm, but which is perhaps more likely to refer to the former Withycombe Farm. Withycombe, which was demolished in the mid-nineteenth century, stood a third of a mile from Culbone Church at the head of the wooded combe which gave the farm a name. A substantial track led in Coleridge's day from Withycombe to the church, and past the farmhouse flowed a noisy brook on its short journey to the sea.[25]

Whatever Coleridge's precise setting during those few days, the autumn landscape of Culbone drew from him an immediate poetic response. To the character Alhadra, a moorish woman in *Osorio*, he gave a lovingly-observed soliloquy which speaks of Somerset not Spain:

> The hanging Woods, that touch'd by Autumn seem'd
> As they were blossoming hues of fire & gold,
> The hanging Woods, most lovely in decay,
> The many clouds, the Sea, the Rock, the Sands,
> Lay in the silent moonshine – and the Owl,
> (Strange, very strange!) the Scritch-owl only wak'd,
> Sole Voice, sole Eye of all that world of Beauty![26]

The other poem which Coleridge wrote during his retreat, and the circumstances of its composition, have entered the mythology of English literary history: while staying at the Culbone farmhouse he took three grains of opium to relieve what he variously described as 'a dysentery' or 'a slight indisposition', and in the deep reverie which followed composed two or three hundred lines of poetry 'without any sensation of consciousness of effort'. Coleridge awoke, he said, retaining 'a distinct recollection of the whole', and was eagerly committing the poem to writing when he was called out by a person on business from Porlock who detained him for more than an hour. When he returned to his room Coleridge was mortified to discover that 'though he still retained some vague and dim recollection of the general purport of the vision, yet, with the exception of some eight or ten scattered lines and images, all the rest had passed away like the images on the surface of a stream into which a stone has been cast . . .'[27]

The story of the poem's composition, though evidently much embellished, is remarkable none the less, the poem itself – 'Kubla Khan' – one of the most remarkable in the language. The primary source for 'Kubla Khan' is the book *Purchas his Pilgrimage* (1614) which Coleridge had evidently brought with him on his Culbone visit – borrowed perhaps from the bookroom or from the well-stocked library at Alfoxden[28] – and which describes how 'In *Xanada* did *Cublai Can* build a stately Pallace.' Other literary sources, including *Paradise Lost*, have been identified with detective zeal, but it was Culbone and Somerset which provided much of the rest. Memories of Cheddar, of Wookey perhaps, echoed through the 'caverns measureless to man', and the Culbone landscape which had

One of the caverns at Wookey Hole, th most spectacular of the Mendip cave systems. Beyond th two standing figures flows the River Axe

inspired his latest writing in *Osorio* now glowed with the imaginative intensity of his opium vision. The setting is unmistakable:

> But oh! that deep romantic chasm which slanted
> Down the green hill athwart a cedarn cover!
> A savage place! as holy and enchanted
> As e'er beneath a waning moon was haunted
> By woman wailing for her demon-lover!
> And from this chasm, with ceaseless turmoil seething,
> As if this earth in fast thick pants were breathing,
> A mighty fountain momently was forced:
> Amid whose swift half-intermitted burst
> Huge fragments vaulted like rebounding hail,

Or chaffy grain beneath the thresher's flail:
And 'mid these dancing rocks at once and ever
It flung up momently the sacred river.

☆

His exalted mood faded as swiftly as his dream. When his few days at Culbone were over, Coleridge descended again into the prosaic lowland world, and by 14 October was home at Lime Street, gloomy and impoverished.

The Ship Inn, Porlock, *c.* 1910. The inn, which Coleridge must have known well, lay on the route from Culbone to Stowey. Southey once sheltered from a storm here, and wrote a bad sonnet 'by the alehouse fire'

Chapter Six

LYRICAL BALLADS

Despite the financial worries with which Coleridge was frequently preoccupied until the end of 1797, he returned from Culbone with at least one cause for celebration. *Osorio* was finished at last, and on 16 October, a few days before his twenty-fifth birthday, he sent a copy of the play, 'complete & neatly transcribed', to William Lisle Bowles in Wiltshire. Coleridge had struggled hard with *Osorio*, and even now he had little faith that it could succeed on stage. But in his relief at having finished the play he scarcely cared about its imperfections. '. . . I feel an indescribable disgust, a sickness of the very heart, at the mention of the Tragedy,' he told Bowles, '. . . I would rather mend hedges & follow the plough, than write another.'[1]

The completion of so large an undertaking suddenly freed Coleridge's creative energy as the days shortened into a rainy winter. In October, following a long silence, he finished two more of the autobiographical letters he had been writing for Tom Poole, providing in one of them, the most deeply-felt of all, his loving recollections of his father, and an account of the stormy night by the River Otter when he had almost died.[2]

It was also in the closing weeks of the year that long explorations of the Somerset landscape by Coleridge and the Wordsworths began to have far-reaching creative consequences. During one excursion which probably occurred at this time Tom Poole took his friends to Walford's Gibbet on the Quantock slopes between Holford and Stowey, and there recounted John Walford's tragic history. Walford, a charcoal-burner who had spent his solitary life in a woodland shelter built of poles and turf, was remembered by Tom Poole as a man 'remarkable for good temper and generosity', but one who also possessed 'ardent feelings and strong passions'. He was deeply in love with an Over Stowey woman called Ann Rice, but was forced into marriage to a half-mad girl who had visited him at his shelter and who bore him two illegitimate children. They married in June 1789, and a month later, in despair and rage, he murdered her as they walked in the darkness to the Castle of Comfort Inn. He was soon arrested, largely through the efforts of Tom Poole's father, and was sentenced to be hanged in chains. Poole remembered that at the place of execution Ann Rice, 'almost lifeless', was brought at John Walford's request from the back of an enormous crowd. She talked with him for nearly ten minutes, and as the officers

The Castle of
Comfort Inn on the
road from Holford
to Nether Stowey

drew her away, Walford snatched her hand and kissed it, 'some tears for the first time rolling down his cheeks'. He admitted the murder in the few words he spoke to the people. 'But I did it without fore-intending it, and I hope God and the world will forgive me.'[3]

On the minds of both Coleridge and Wordsworth the story of John Walford made a deep impression. It was a reminder that the Quantocks were not merely nature's beautiful and benevolent face, but the setting also of great tragedy, where the extremes of human emotion found expression in the humblest lives. Some of Wordsworth's most radical contributions to the *Lyrical Ballads* were to explore the tragic experience of country people, and John Walford's story was itself used by Wordsworth as the subject of a substantial poem. But the unpublished manuscript, given to Tom Poole, was destroyed in 1931 by Gordon Words-worth, who evidently regarded the subject of adultery and murder as too sordid even for the twentieth century.[4] The effect on Coleridge of what Tom Poole had told them both was perhaps of most significance. John Walford's fate spoke powerfully of life's arbitrary horror, and of destruction brought down on a good and generous man who had done a terrible thing, but 'without fore-intending it'. Such ideas were to preoccupy Coleridge as the year drew to a close.

Other more ambitious walks also took place that winter. In early November Coleridge and the Wordsworths, whose deep and intuitive friendship had begun by now to exclude not only Sara but even Tom Poole, set out on the road to

The Valley of the
Rocks, *c*. 1850

Porlock which Coleridge had taken the previous month. Coleridge introduced
his friends to the steep woodland track leading from Porlock Weir to Culbone,
and together they walked on for four miles beneath the trees, before emerging
close to Broomstreet Farm and Yenworthy. By dusk Lynmouth had been
reached, and next morning they went the short distance to the Valley of the
Rocks, a strange and desolate dry valley running parallel to the coast and
bordered by great castellated tors of rock. The landscape of the valley was quickly
reproduced in an unfinished prose tale, 'The Wanderings of Cain', a story of
murder and remorse whose details were discussed on this November tour. It was
decided that Wordsworth should write the first book or canto of the tale,
Coleridge the second, 'and which ever had *done first*, was to set about the third'.
But the collaboration was a predictable failure, and Coleridge, having written his
own canto 'at full finger-speed', found Wordsworth seated before a nearly blank
sheet of paper with a look of 'humorous despondency' on his face.[5] A second

The Great Track at
Holford Beeches, on
the Quantock Hills
above Alfoxden,
photographed *c.* 1930

attempt at joint composition followed almost at once, in the course of another tour, and although the two friends were no more successful than before at direct collaboration, a new and remarkable poem began to emerge none the less. Coleridge proposed to call it 'The Rime of the Ancient Mariner'.

☆

The walking tour during which 'The Ancient Mariner' was planned and partly written began in failing light on 13 November 1797. Setting out from Alfoxden at half-past four, Coleridge and the Wordsworths followed the Great Track over the Quantock Hills, and as they marched westward through a 'dark and cloudy'

Castle Hill House, Nether Stowey, the home of John Cruikshank, who probably had his dream of a spectre ship here

evening, agreed that a poem should be written for publication to cover the expenses of their journey. It was to be a ballad based on the supernatural, as were other popular ballads of the time, and would retell in lively narrative and simple verse form an old mariner's hypnotic tale. Coleridge and Wordsworth felt confident that the *Monthly Magazine* would give £5 for the poem, and they were already discussing details of the plot as they descended from the hills at West Quantoxhead. Immediate inspiration was provided by Coleridge's memory of a conversation with John Cruikshank, his Stowey friend, who had recently recounted his disturbing dream of a spectre ship. To this element of the developing story Wordsworth soon added several more, as he still remembered over forty years later:

. . . For example, some crime was to be committed which would bring upon the Old Navigator, as Coleridge afterwards delighted to call him, the spectral persecution . . . and his own wanderings. I had been reading in Shelvocke's *Voyages*, a day or two before, that, while doubling Cape Horn, they frequently saw albatrosses in that latitude, the largest sort of sea-fowl . . . 'Suppose,' said I, 'you represent him as having killed one of these birds on entering the South Sea, and that the tutelary spirits of these regions take upon them to avenge the crime.' The incident was thought fit for the purpose, and adopted accordingly.

The harbour at Watchet, *c.* 1750. Painting probably by Robert Griffier

Some further details of the poem were clearly borrowed directly from West Somerset: the harbour from which the mariner set sail can only be the little harbour at Watchet, the hermit's woodland home the wood at Culbone, and the 'loud bassoon', whose sound caused the wedding-guest to beat his breast, probably had its original in the bassoon which the vicar of Stowey had just provided for the Stowey church band.[6]

'We began the composition together,' Wordsworth recalled, 'on that to me memorable evening.' But although Wordsworth contributed a few lines, he quickly realized that attempts at collaboration were once again bound to fail: '. . . Our respective manners proved so widely different, that it would have been quite presumptuous in me to do anything but separate from an undertaking upon which I could only have been a clog.' They probably stayed that night at Watchet, and there, tradition records, the first lines of 'The Ancient Mariner' were committed to writing at the Bell Inn, within sight of the ships in Watchet's decaying harbour. The route they followed on leaving the town is not known in

The Bell Inn,
Watchet, *c*. 1910.
Tradition says that
'The Ancient
Mariner' was begun
here

detail. It is certain only that they passed through Dulverton, and within a week were home once more, bringing with them 'many pleasant, and some of them droll enough, recollections'.[7]

Coleridge made rapid progress with the poem, and almost as soon as he reached Stowey he was writing to Joseph Cottle with news of a ballad 'of about 300 lines'.[8] 'The Ancient Mariner' was finally to reach more than twice that length, but even in its early form had clearly developed beyond its original purpose as a magazine ballad. Having gathered up the elements of his story from Wordsworth and John Cruikshank, Coleridge had, in a week of brilliant creativity, produced not a gothic ballad of the supernatural, but a strange and

Illustration by
Gustav Doré for
edition of 'The
Ancient Mariner',
1877

capacious metaphor of life itself – of man's lonely voyage on a 'wide wide sea', of his struggle with evil, of guilt and imperfect redemption. Not least, perhaps, the mariner's story spoke of man's tragic and childlike vulnerability to forces of destruction both from within himself and beyond. That was a truth which John Walford's gibbet continued to proclaim a short distance from the Stowey road, and which Coleridge's own opium-addicted future would bitterly confirm.

Neither Coleridge nor the Wordsworths were in any doubt that 'The Ancient Mariner' was a work of great power and originality, a poem, as Coleridge later said, which could not be imitated. On 20 November, when Dorothy wrote to a friend, talk of the *Monthly Magazine* had been forgotten. Instead, they were now proposing that the poem should appear, 'with some pieces of William's', in a volume of its own.[9]

The creative preoccupations of November yielded at year's end to familiar concerns about money and the future. In London during December the Words-worths learned that both *The Borderers* and *Osorio* had been rejected, and Coleridge at home in Lime Street wondered more than ever how and where he was to earn a living. A letter from Shrewsbury, received in Christmas week, provided one possible answer. The Unitarian congregation in the town was shortly to lose its minister, and had written on the recommendation of John Prior Estlin to ask if Coleridge would agree to be considered as successor. Coleridge told Estlin that his heart 'yearned toward the ministry', and he was soon able to convince himself that even his unorthodox beliefs might not be a major obstacle to his acceptance of the post, and the income it would guarantee.[10]

On the same day that he heard of the post at Shrewsbury, however, another letter reached him, addressed in an unfamiliar hand. It came from Thomas and Josiah Wedgwood – rich sons of the famous potter – to whom Coleridge had recently been introduced by Tom Poole. Their letter enclosed a quite unexpected gift of £100, a sum more than sufficient to free him from the immediate necessity of hard choices, and a testimony of their faith in his genius. 'My friend T. Poole', Coleridge wrote, 'strenuously advised me to accept it.' But on 5 January, 'after much & very painful hesitation', he sent the money back, expressing at the same time 'no ordinary feelings of esteem and affection' for his benefactors. He had decided in favour of Shrewsbury, if the congregation there were willing to appoint him.[11]

Coleridge arrived in the town late on Saturday 13 January, and on the following day preached two trial sermons in the Unitarian chapel. He wrote laconically that night to John Prior Estlin, leaving unstated the bewilderment he evidently felt as he prepared to exchange Somerset for Shropshire. 'It is chilling to go among *strangers*,' he had written a few days earlier, '& I leave a lovely country.'[12] If his mood was gloomy, that was not immediately apparent to one

William Hazlitt
(1778–1830) as a
young man. From a
portrait by John
Hazlitt

member of his morning congregation. William Hazlitt, the nineteen-year-old son
of the minister at Wem, had walked ten miles through the winter mud to hear the
preaching of the now-celebrated poet and philosopher.[13] It was an occasion he
never forgot:

> When I got there, the organ was playing the 100th psalm, and, when it was
> done, Mr Coleridge rose and gave out his text, 'And he went up into the
> mountain to pray, HIMSELF ALONE.' As he gave out his text, his voice 'rose like
> a steam of rich distilled perfumes,' and when he came to the two last words,
> which he pronounced loud, deep, and distinct, it seemed to me, who was then
> young, as if the sounds had echoed from the bottom of the human heart, and as
> if that prayer might have floated in solemn silence through the universe.

Two days later Coleridge visited the Hazlitts at Wem, and the diffident,
admiring son of the house listened in awe as 'the half-inspired speaker' pronounced on Mary Wollstonecraft, Godwin, and Burke. Hazlitt carefully
observed the visitor's appearance – the broad, high forehead, the projecting
eyebrows, and the dark, rolling eyes. 'His mouth was gross, voluptuous, open,
eloquent; his chin good-humoured and round; but his nose, the rudder of the
face, the index of the will, was small, feeble, nothing . . .'. It was next morning

that Hazlitt came down to breakfast to find Coleridge with a letter he had just received from the Wedgwoods. The brothers were now offering an annuity for life of £150, 'no condition whatsoever being annexed to it'. Presented with so ready a means of escape from a course of action whose wisdom he already doubted, Coleridge's decision was predictable and eager. He thought briefly, and then, Hazlitt recalled, 'seemed to make up his mind to close with this proposal in the act of tying on one of his shoes'. Hazlitt set out with Coleridge that morning on the road back to Shrewsbury, observing how his companion continually moved from one side of the footpath to the other as they walked along, though only later connecting this odd movement with 'any instability of purpose or involuntary change of principle'. Coleridge talked incessantly, and 'in digressing, in dilating, in passing from subject to subject', he appeared to 'float in air, to slide on ice'. He had already invited his new young friend to travel to Stowey a few weeks later, and when they parted after six miles, Hazlitt was possessed by a single thought: '*I was to visit Coleridge in the spring.*'

For eleven more days Coleridge remained at Shrewsbury, elated by his sudden freedom from 'all pecuniary anxieties', and longing to be home in Somerset. He travelled back by way of Westbury-on-Trym, where he paid his personal thanks to the Wedgwood brothers at Cote House. From Shrewsbury a few days earlier he had already written to Tom Poole:

> I wish to be at home with you indeed, indeed – my Joy is only in the bud here – I am like that Tree, which fronts me – The Sun shines bright & warm, as if it were summer – but it is not summer & so it shines on leafless boughs. The beings who know how to sympathize with me are my foliage.[14]

When Coleridge and the Wordsworths met together once more after a separation of several weeks, it was in the knowledge that the Alfoxden year would soon be over. They seem, in the months that followed, to have lived with a new intensity, half-knowing that their shared joy in creativity and friendship might never be repeated. For Coleridge and Wordsworth the publication in October of the *Lyrical Ballads* was a lasting commemoration of their year together. Dorothy's own attempt to preserve something from those final Somerset months produced a document more private, but hardly less remarkable. On a Saturday in late January 1798, sitting perhaps at one of the tall windows in her favourite parlour, she began the first of her surviving journals:

> ALFOXDEN, *January 20th 1798.* – The green paths down the hill-sides are channels for streams. The young wheat is streaked by silver lines of water running between the ridges, the sheep are gathered together on the slopes. After the wet dark days, the country seems more populous. It peoples itself in the sunbeams.[15]

Cote House,
Westbury-on-Trym,
the 'magnificent
Seat' of John
Wedgwood, brother
of Josiah and Tom

Her response to nature had a subtlety beyond the range either of her brother or of Coleridge, and indeed was a response altogether different from theirs. She showed a profound deference to the beauty she described, never searching for meaning or metaphor in the landscape, never striving to achieve what Keats would later call the 'wordsworthian or egotistical sublime'. For her it was sufficient that the Quantock sheep glittered with dew in the morning sunshine, that the full moon rose 'in uncommon majesty' over the sea, and that the silk-weaver's dog howled in the dark at the sound of the village stream. Both Coleridge and Wordsworth recognized their great indebtedness to Dorothy – 'watchful in minutest observation of nature' – and borrowed freely from her in their poetry.[16]

Dorothy's journal makes it clear that the three friends were now in each other's company almost daily. They walked in the deer park and its surrounding beech woods; they followed the lanes to Putsham, Holford and Crowcombe; and they were drawn repeatedly to the sea at Kilve and into the Quantocks. On an afternoon in late February they climbed to the great Iron Age hill-fort at Dowsborough, from where they looked down on 'a magnificent scene, *curiously* spread out for even minute inspection'; and on other occasions they watched from the hills as the effects of the weather unfolded over the landscape below. 'I never saw such a union of earth, sky, and sea,' Dorothy wrote following one

View from
Dowsborough hil[l]
fort towards the
estuary of the Riv[er]
Parrett, *c.* 1900.
After a painting [by]
William Hyde

hill-top walk. 'The clouds beneath our feet spread themselves to the water, and the clouds of the sky almost joined them.'[17]

While Dorothy was making the first entries in her journal that new year Coleridge continued to write poetry with undiminished fluency, both at Stowey and Alfoxden. He worked furiously to revise and expand 'The Ancient Mariner', and on a night in February wrote a poem of wonderful beauty addressed to his infant son. 'Frost at Midnight', perhaps the finest of the Conversation Poems, is a meditation on Coleridge's own childhood, and a passionate expression of hope for Hartley's future. It is set in the Lime Street parlour, where Coleridge sits by the 'low-burnt' parlour fire, and Hartley, his 'cradled infant', sleeps beside him. The Somerset landscape has been dissolved in darkness, and the mysterious forces of nature, normally sought by Coleridge high in the Quantocks, or in the dell at Alfoxden, now wash over the sleeping town and reach to the very door of his cottage. As the frost descends, and in its 'secret ministry' of transformation makes icicles along the dripping eaves, Coleridge's meditative mind carries him

One of the parlours at the Lime Street cottage as it appears today. Coleridge's inkstand is at the centre of the table

to the scenes of his childhood, and imagines for Hartley a future, not in the 'great city', but 'beneath the crags/Of ancient mountain, and beneath the clouds'. In the poem's final radiant lines, his thoughts remain with Hartley, but are linked now to an evocation of the natural world of Stowey in all its beauty, even the strange beauty at work outside his cottage that February midnight, where 'silent icicles' are 'Quietly shining to the quiet Moon'.

Coleridge must soon have taken the poem to read to the Wordsworths, and in the following month had an even more substantial achievement to show them. On a day which was among the more remarkable in literary history, he set out from Lime Street, and as on so many previous occasions reached Alfoxden down the lonely tree-shuttered lane through the deer park. He had brought with him the completed manuscript of 'The Ancient Mariner', and read it to the Wordsworths for the first time, so tradition says, in one of the Alfoxden parlours. The date was 23 March 1798. That night the Wordsworths walked back with him as

JACQUIDIE AVENUE   N A RIXON. 99

far as the miner's house, a short distance from the beech tree above Woodlands Farm where they often parted. 'A beautiful evening,' Dorothy noted. 'Very starry, the horned moon.'[18]

☆

By the time 'The Ancient Mariner' was finally complete, Coleridge and Wordsworth were already clarifying their plans for publishing a joint volume of poetry. Discussions on the subject had begun late in November, when the 'old navigator' had first became part of their lives, but Dorothy's remark at the end of their walking tour that Coleridge's poem would appear 'with some pieces of William's' was followed by a long silence. Only after Coleridge returned from Shrewsbury, freed at last from immediate financial worry, could vague hopes be transformed into clearer intentions.

Money to help pay for ambitious future plans was at least one motive for seeking publication. In early March, during a long visit to the Wordsworths made by Coleridge and Sara – now heavily pregnant with her second child – it was decided that once Alfoxden had been given up, they should all set sail from England and travel in Germany. The impetus for suggesting so major an upheaval came from Coleridge, who felt an increasing sense of obligation to live up to the hopes so clearly implied by the Wedgwood annuity. In Germany, the pre-eminent centre of Europe's intellectual life, he could not only learn the language, but engage in the study of philosophy and religion which he now felt certain was his true vocation. '. . . Money is necessary to our plan,' he was soon telling Joseph Cottle; and from a volume of poems they might raise sixty guineas.[19]

At first Cottle was asked to consider a new edition of *Poems on Various Subjects*, or a volume of Wordsworth's poems, or perhaps a joint edition of *Osorio* and *The Borderers*. Finally, the thoughts of the two poets tended towards a volume of another kind, which would reflect the poetic concerns of their many conversations since the beginning of the Alfoxden year. Those conversations, Coleridge remembered, 'turned frequently on the two cardinal points of poetry, the power of exciting the sympathy of the reader by a faithful adherence to the truth of nature, and the power of giving the interest of novelty by the modifying colours of imagination'. These 'cardinal points', they now proposed, should find expression through a series of experimental poems in which Coleridge was to concern himself with subjects 'supernatural, or at least romantic', and Wordsworth was to 'give the charm of novelty to things of every day', seeking for characters and incidents 'such . . . as will be found in every village'. It was from these tentative beginnings that the *Lyrical Ballads* finally emerged.[20]

Wordsworth was soon writing verse with greater confidence than ever before. 'His faculties seem to expand every day,' Dorothy wrote in early March; 'he composes with much more facility than he did, as to the *mechanism* of poetry, and

The oak tree in th
grounds at Alfoxd
traditionally said t
be the 'huge oak
tree' mentioned in
part one of
Coleridge's poem
'Christabel'

his ideas flow faster than he can express them.'[21] Most of the poems Wordsworth contributed to the *Lyrical Ballads* were completed in an astonishing burst of creativity during the next few weeks, and drew their inspiration largely from his immediate surroundings at Holford and Alfoxden. Christopher Tricky, seen struggling one day to remove an old tree stump near his hovel at the park gate, became, as has already been noted, the subject of 'Simon Lee, the Old Huntsman'; a remark from Tom Poole led to 'The Idiot Boy'; 'The Last of the Flock' told the story of a Holford shepherd found weeping in the road; and 'The Thorn' was inspired by a weather-beaten hawthorn seen 'on the ridge of Quantock Hill'.[22] The studied plainness of diction in these poems of country life was an important part of their experimental character, but became the object of much ridicule. A few more meditative poems, however, achieved a lyrical power which disarmed most critics, and which helped some early readers, such as the young Thomas De Quincey, to see in the collection as a whole that 'ray of a new morning' which marked the beginning of English Romanticism. One hastily-written poem in Wordsworth's meditative manner, 'Lines Written at a Small Distance from my House', was delivered to Dorothy by young Basil as the Quantock spring was at last arriving:

> It is the first mild day of March:
> Each minute sweeter than before,
> The red-breast sings from the tall larch
> That stands beside our door.
>
> There is a blessing in the air,
> Which seems a sense of joy to yield
> To the bare trees, and mountains bare,
> And grass in the green field . . .

☆

Some of the new poetry Coleridge intended for the joint volume was not written with nearly such ease. In the first weeks of the year he had probably begun 'Christabel', an ambitious medieval romance founded once more on supernatural events. But the poem remained unfinished, a consequence, he later said, of the vindictive ill will which Charles Lloyd had begun to show towards him, perhaps with encouragement from Robert Southey. A novel by Lloyd, called *Edmund Oliver*, appeared in April, and contained a thinly-disguised and unflattering portrait of Coleridge which deeply offended and disturbed him.[23]

When the *Lyrical Ballads* finally appeared, Coleridge's contributions, other than 'The Ancient Mariner', amounted to no more than two extracts from *Osorio*, and a Conversation Poem called 'The Nightingale', which was written during April. 'The Nightingale' provides a record of one of the evening walks shared by Coleridge and the Wordsworths which had been so much a part of their lives together. They rest on an 'old mossy bridge', probably at Holford, and listen to the singing of the 'merry Nightingale', before they say farewell in the darkness and turn for their homes. Another poem, 'Fears in Solitude', was also completed that April, and was probably Coleridge's last substantial poem of the Alfoxden year. Set in a 'green and silent spot, amid the hills', it was not intended for the *Lyrical Ballads*, but was a political meditation inspired by fears of a French invasion. Coleridge declares loyalty to his country but contempt for its governors, and then ends the poem, as he begins it, with the Somerset landscape. He follows a hill-track on his journey home, and looks out with startled pleasure when the coastal plain emerges below him. There seems a note of valediction in the loving intensity of his description, a desire to record for one last time the scenes which, for more than a year, had so filled his mind and shaped his thoughts:

> . . . And after lonely sojourning
> In such a quiet and surrounded nook,
> This burst of prospect, here the shadowy main,
> Dim-tinted, there the mighty majesty
> Of that huge amphitheatre of rich
> And elmy fields, seems like society –
> Conversing with the mind, and giving it
> A livelier impulse and a dance of thought!
> And now, beloved Stowey! I behold
> Thy church-tower, and, methinks, the four huge elms
> Clustering, which mark the mansion of my friend;
> And close behind them, hidden from my view,
> Is my own lowly cottage, where my babe
> And my babe's mother dwell in peace! . . .

As he looked out over the familiar landscape that spring day, the poetic miracles which had begun in the lime-tree bower were coming to an end.

View from the Quantock Hills towards Minehead and Exmoor, 1890

124

St Mary's Church,
Nether Stowey.
Tom Poole is buried
near the church door

William Hazlitt's visit to Somerset, so eagerly anticipated since January, began in fine summer weather towards the end of May.[24] Having made the journey from Shropshire more quickly than he expected, he lingered nervously at Bridgwater for two days. But once he reached Stowey the Coleridges greeted him warmly at Lime Street, where the cottage had gained another new resident only a week before: on 14 May, Sara had been 'safely delivered of a fine boy', the child being given the name Berkeley in honour of the philosopher, for whom Coleridge was developing a great admiration.[25]

When Hazlitt and Coleridge visited Alfoxden the following day, Wordsworth was away from home; but Dorothy provided them with a 'frugal repast' and let them see the now-abundant manuscripts intended for the *Lyrical Ballads*. They stayed the night at Alfoxden, Hazlitt sleeping in a room filled with 'round-faced family-portraits' of the St Albyns, and waking next morning to the bellowing of a Quantock stag. After breakfast, he and Coleridge walked in the park, taking Wordsworth's manuscripts with them:

. . . Seating ourselves on the trunk of an old ash-tree that stretched along the ground, Coleridge read aloud with a sonorous and musical voice, the ballad of *Betty Foy*. I was not critically or sceptically inclined. I saw touches of truth and nature, and took the rest for granted. But in the *Thorn*, the *Mad Mother*, and the

Alfoxden, *c.* 189

Complaint of a Poor Indian Woman, I felt that deeper power and pathos which have been since acknowledged . . . as the characteristics of this author; and the sense of a new style and a new spirit in poetry came over me. It had to me something of the effect that arises from the turning up of the fresh soil, or of the first welcome breath of Spring.

In the evening they walked home to Stowey in the summer moonlight – 'through echoing grove, by fairy stream or waterfall' – Coleridge lamenting that Wordsworth was unwilling to believe in local superstitions, 'and that there was a something corporeal, *a matter-of-fact-ness*, a clinging to the palpable, or often to the petty, in his poetry, in consequence'. Wordsworth himself arrived at Lime

Street the following day, quaintly dressed, as Hazlitt remembered, in a brown fustian jacket and striped pantaloons, and talking freely in his strong northern accent:

> Wordsworth, looking out of the low, latticed window, said, 'How beautifully the sun sets on that yellow bank!' I thought within myself, 'With what eyes these poets see nature!' and ever after, when I saw the sun-set stream upon the objects facing it, conceived I had made a discovery, or thanked Mr Wordsworth for having made one for me!

The shy young visitor was soon disputing with Wordsworth almost on equal terms; and next evening, while Coleridge was providing Dorothy with super-fluous explanations about the different notes of the nightingale, Hazlitt and Wordsworth 'got into a metaphysical argument' which may have inspired two of the most genial of the *Lyrical Ballads* – 'Expostulation and Reply', and 'The Tables Turned', both of them written 'in front of the house at Alfoxden'.[26]

Hazlitt relished a long summer walk to the Valley of the Rocks, undertaken with Coleridge and John Chester, a farmer's son from Dodington. Chester, who was soon to accompany Coleridge on the journey into Europe, was yet another who had been drawn to him 'as flies are to honey', and now trotted happily beside his two talkative companions, bow-legged and awestruck. They passed close to Dunster, which lay beneath a wooded hill looking 'as clear, as pure, as *embrowned*'

Dunster village and castle, 1820

as a Poussin landscape. At Broomstreet Farm Hazlitt called 'The Ancient Mariner' to their minds by pointing to the bare masts of a ship, outlined against 'the red-orbed disk of the setting sun'. And at the Valley of the Rocks, he remembered, Coleridge rushed from the inn when a thunderstorm threatened, 'to enjoy the commotion of the elements'.

It was probably in the course of Hazlitt's three-week visit that Joseph Cottle also arrived, finally persuaded by Coleridge and Wordsworth that he should travel down to spend a few days discussing the intended volume of poetry. Its contents were still very much in doubt when Cottle reached Alfoxden; but before his visit ended the famous title had been chosen, and the decision made that the volume should begin with 'The Ancient Mariner' and include 'sundry shorter poems' of Wordsworth's, most of them written since the beginning of the year. The volume was to be anonymous, since, as Coleridge explained, 'Wordsworth's name is nothing – to a large number of persons mine *stinks*'. At the end of May Dorothy could write to her brother Richard that 'William has now some poems in the Bristol press'; and by mid-September, just as Coleridge and Wordsworth were preparing to leave for Germany, the *Lyrical Ballads* were at last ready to be offered to an indifferent public.[27]

Those last high-spirited weeks at Alfoxden and Stowey were almost at an end by the time Cottle and Hazlitt left for home. In the little time that remained, plans for Germany were made, and no doubt farewell visits took the three friends by now-familiar routes to the beach at Kilve, to Holford Combe and Hodder's Combe, and far into the hills. Finally, on Saturday 23 June, the Wordsworths left Alfoxden, and went for the last time down the wooded lane through the deer park, past the beech trees and hollies where, on a day in March, they had sheltered from a hail storm, past Christopher Tricky's hovel near the dog pound, and past the 'loud Waterfall', whose sound would always echo in their memories. Dorothy had 'not often felt more regret' than she did that day.[28]

For a week they stayed at the Lime Street cottage, where Sara was already doubting the wisdom of taking part in the German expedition. As the mother of two small children, the youngest hardly a month old, her eventual decision to remain at Stowey was clearly sensible. But the months of separation from her husband, and the events those months contained, came to mark a fundamental breach in their relationship, after which there ceased to be any hope that their early married happiness could be recovered.

By early July the Wordsworths had taken up temporary residence at Cottle's house in Wine Street, Bristol, where Dorothy found the noise of the Bristol streets almost intolerable. 'You can scarcely conceive', she wrote, 'how the jarring contrast between the sounds which are now for-ever ringing in my ears and the sweet sounds of Allfoxden makes me long for the country again.'[29] An opportunity for escape occurred shortly afterwards when she and Wordsworth set off on a walking tour into the Wye Valley. Wordsworth's poetic fluency had never been greater, and the landscape near Tintern Abbey, revisited after an

Holford Combe

absence of five years, released from him a stream of meditative blank verse quite different in style from the humble poems of rural life he had been writing for the *Lyrical Ballads*. 'Lines Written a Few Miles above Tintern Abbey' is a poem in Wordsworth's loftiest philosophical manner, and a triumphant affirmation of God's creative and restorative power at work in nature. 'No poem of mine was composed under circumstances more pleasant for me to remember than this,' Wordsworth wrote.

I began it upon leaving Tintern, after crossing the Wye, and concluded it just as I was entering Bristol in the evening, after a ramble of four or five days, with my sister. Not a line of it was altered, and not any part of it written down till I reached Bristol.[30]

Tintern Abbey,
c. 1830

Cottle's home in Wine Street was probably the setting in which 'Tintern Abbey' reached written form, and almost at once it was chosen to take a place of honour as the last of the *Lyrical Ballads*. The poem was the finest Wordsworth had yet written, and, coming so soon after his departure from Alfoxden, suggests that the loss to him of the Quantock countryside had been of little real significance. Although his years at Racedown and Alfoxden had seen the growth of his vocation as a poet, his geographical loyalties lay elsewhere, and it was in the north that his future life, and many of his greatest poetic achievements, would be set. For Coleridge, the West Country man, the decision to leave for Germany had a more profound importance. As he took the road to Bridgwater with John Chester, something essential to his happiness remained behind him, both in the rich and various landscape which so closely mirrored the landscape of his mind, and in the generous steadying friendship of Tom Poole. Sara's continued presence in the Lime Street cottage meant that he would inevitably return to Stowey, however briefly; but his departure in the late summer of 1798 was in most senses final.

Stowey Court and the gazebo, on the road from Nether Stowey to Bridgwater. From a watercolour by John Buckler, 1840

The four travellers arrived in Yarmouth on 15 September, young Basil having been left, with much sadness, in the care of his family in London. To Tom Poole that day, Coleridge wrote a farewell letter, setting down his sense of all that Poole had been to him since the beginning of their friendship more than four years earlier:

Of many friends, whom I love and esteem, my head & heart have ever chosen you as the Friend – as the one being, in whom is involved the full & whole meaning of that sacred Title – God love you, my dear Poole! and your faithful & most affectionate

S T Coleridge

Then, in a postscript, as if feeling that his measured words had not yet said enough, he added with a sudden note of desperation: 'May God preserve us & make us continue to be joy & comfort & wisdom & virtue to each other, my dear, dear, Poole!'[31]

On Sunday morning, 16 September, they set sail in the packet-boat on a boisterous sea.[32] Chester and the Wordsworths were violently seasick almost at once. But Coleridge found that he rather enjoyed the rolling of the deck, and held long and facetious conversations with a talkative fellow passenger. Very soon the coast of England had vanished in the distance.

Chapter Seven

'I FEEL WHAT I HAVE LOST'

Coleridge had no clear sense of what the future held for him as the packet-boat pitched its way over the North Sea that September morning. Originally he and the Wordsworths had talked of spending two years in Germany; but by the time they sailed from Yarmouth, Coleridge was intending a visit of no more than three or four months, to be extended only if Sara and the children eventually followed him abroad. In the meantime, he promised letters twice a week, alternately to Sara and Tom Poole, and began his first long letter home as soon as the boat reached the German coast. 'When we lost sight of land,' he wrote to Sara, 'the moment that we quite lost sight of it, & the heavens all round me rested upon the waters, my dear Babies came upon me like a flash of lightening – I saw their faces so distinctly!'[1]

His letters to Stowey in the coming months charted his progress first to Hamburg, then to Ratzeburg, and in the new year to the university city of Göttingen, where he entered with enthusiasm into the vigorous intellectual life he found. The Wordsworths had decided to separate from him almost as soon as they arrived in Germany: having discovered that the price of lodgings was unexpectedly high, they left their friend to his studious but very social life, and settled as cheaply as they could in the town of Goslar, at the foot of the Harz Mountains. There, in congenial solitude, a further period of intense creativity began for Wordsworth.

First word from Stowey came in a letter written during October by Tom Poole. There was, he said, almost no news to report, and the only excitement to have disturbed the town since Coleridge's departure had been the celebration for Nelson's victory at the Battle of the Nile. What Tom Poole deliberately failed to say, however, was that all was far from well with Coleridge's family. At the cottage in Lime Street Berkeley was on the brink of death, having been inoculated with smallpox, and, like many children of the period, been made dangerously ill with the disease in consequence. Poole convinced Sara that the news should be kept from her husband until the worst was known, and through a series of accidents with the post, her agonized account of Berkeley's sufferings did not reach Coleridge until late November.[2]

For days Berkeley had lain in Sara's lap like a dead child, burning with fever, and had quickly become almost entirely covered with pock-marks. 'He was blind

132

The *Zwinger*, one of the defensive towers of the town of Goslar, Lower Saxony. It was in Goslar that Wordsworth wrote the 'Lucy' poems, as well as parts of *The Prelude*

– his nose was clogged that he could not suck and his dear gums and tongue were covered.' Whenever she dozed for a moment the '*horrid noise*' in his throat came to her in her dreams. But slowly he began to recover, and by the time Sara wrote to her husband on 1 November, the worst danger seemed to have passed. Then, late on 20 November, Berkeley was taken ill once more, this time with 'suffocation and fever', and a week later developed a violent cough. Sara was distracted. For weeks she had borne 'an agony of care' without Coleridge's support, and when she wrote on 13 December she told him that she looked 'at least ten years older' than when they had parted.[3]

She took Berkeley to Mrs Fricker's house in Bristol at the end of the year, in hopes that a change of air would do good. Instead, Berkeley grew ever more thin and weak, and, on 10 February 1799, he died. Sara wrote immediately to one of the only friends on whom she could now rely:

Oh! my dear Mr Poole, I have lost my dear dear child! at one o'clock on Sunday Morning a violent convulsive fit put an end to his painful existance, myself and two of his aunts were watching by his cradle. I wish I had not seen it, for I am sure it will never leave my memory; sweet babe! what will thy Father feel when he shall hear of thy sufferings and death!

133

Berkeley was found to have died of consumption, evidently caught from the Coleridges' servant, Nanny, who was in the advanced stages of the disease. Robert Southey arranged for the child's burial, and at this great crisis of Sara's life showed the strength of character she would always admire in him, and which now seemed in such marked contrast to the character of her husband.[4]

Poole was determined to protect the susceptible Coleridge from the full truth of the catastrophe which had overtaken his family, and cruelly misrepresented Sara's deep distress when finally he sent news that Berkeley had died. 'Mrs. Coleridge was much fatigued during the child's illness,' he wrote, 'but her health was very good, and she very wisely kept up her spirits. . . .' Coleridge, in reply, was philosophic and calm:

> I cannot truly say that I grieve – I am perplexed – I am sad – and a little thing, a very trifle would make me weep; but for the death of the Baby I have *not* wept! – Oh! this strange, strange, strange Scene-shifter, Death!

Now, at least, he began to talk seriously of his plans for returning home. In a letter written to Sara on 23 April he said that he hoped to be in England 'this day in June', and wished that he could reach land at the desolate Shurton Bars and walk back to her along the lanes to Stowey. 'It lessens the delight of the thought of my Return, that I must get at you thro' a tribe of *acquaintances, damping* the freshness of one's Joy!' But in spite of the homesickness he continued to profess both to Sara and Tom Poole, feelings of guilt, and the pleasurable distractions of Germany, prevented his return to England for three more months. Only in late July, ten months after his departure, was he home again in Lime Street.[5]

Sara's justifiable sense that Coleridge had abandoned her when she most needed him cannot have made the home-coming an easy one. The strains in their relationship became increasingly apparent in the months ahead, and disagreements seem to have begun almost at once. It was probably at Sara's angry insistence that Coleridge, soon after reaching Stowey, wrote a brief and embarrassed letter to Robert Southey, then on holiday in Minehead, asking that they should resume at least 'the outward Expressions of daily Kindliness' in their relationship with one another. Sara had benefited too much from Southey's generous help in recent months to have patience with what she considered to be her husband's unreasonable dislike, and after a second letter from Coleridge, and one from Tom Poole, the reconciliation was finally achieved. The two men embraced at the door of the cottage in Lime Street when the Southeys returned from Minehead, and shortly afterwards, with peace restored, the whole party set off together on a journey into Devon.[6]

☆

The Devon journey of 1799 was for Sara a welcome distraction from the painful experiences of recent months, and became for Coleridge the occasion of his final visit to Ottery St Mary. His brother James ('the Colonel') had by now taken up residence at the Chanter's House – still the home of his descendants – and George had succeeded to his father's old post as master of the King's School. The visit was a happy one, and Sara was delighted by the kindness with which she was received. But Coleridge, even though he had by now entirely turned his back on radical politics, could not fail to see that his opinions on most subjects had drifted far from those of his family. 'I have three Brothers,' he wrote to Tom Poole in September; '. . . two are Parsons and one is a Colonel – George & the Colonel good men as times go – very good men; but alas! we have neither Tastes or Feelings in common. This I wisely learnt from their Conversation; & did not suffer them to learn it from *mine*.' He drank toasts to Church and King without a word of dissent, and considered the generous supply of 'Roast Fowls, mealy Potatoes, Pies, & Clouted Cream' with which his hosts provided him as reason enough to keep his views to himself.[7] Southey was greatly amused one day when old Mrs Coleridge was present with her sons: 'She could not hear what was going on, but seeing Samuel arguing with his brothers, took it for granted that he must have been wrong, and cried out, 'Ah, if your poor father had been alive, he'd soon have convinced you!'[8]

The Convention Room, or parlour, at the Chanter's House, Ottery St Mary, where Colonel James Coleridge entertained his brother Samuel in 1799

Hartley Coleridge
(1796–1849) at the
age of ten. After a
portrait by Sir David
Wilkie

The contented interlude which the Devon visit provided in the relationship of Coleridge and Sara quickly came to an end. Hartley appeared to have caught the 'Itch' from the new family servant, Fanny (who was quickly dispensed with), and when the Coleridges returned to Lime Street, Sara was 'tired off her legs' fumigating the house and washing bedclothes. Soon she was forced to call on the help of her kindly neighbour, Mrs Rich, in order to cope at all. Only Hartley rather enjoyed the commotion, and when he was anointed with brimstone sang the little rhyme, 'I be a funny Fellow, And my name is Brimstonello.' Coleridge, who was suffering from an attack of rheumatism after walking in the rain, retreated miserably to a corner, and there, 'undisturbed as a Toad in a Rock', he spent his days reading Spinoza.[9]

Humour flashed intermittently in the gloomy cottage. When Tom Ward, Poole's assistant at Castle Street, sent over a promised batch of pens, Coleridge thanked him for his kindness in a letter overflowing with bad puns: 'Were I to write till *Pen*tecost,' he concluded, 'filling whole *Pen*tateuchs, my grateful Expressions would still remain merely a *Pen*umbra of my Debt & Gratitude.' More often, anger and resentment prevailed at Lime Street as the incomprehension between husband and wife deepened into silence. On 15 September 1799 Coleridge wrote to Southey that, 'Sara & I go to Bristol in a few days.' In the

event, he walked off alone, and turned his back on a cottage whose inconveniences and associations had become intolerable to him. He was never to live under its dilapidated roof again.[10]

Coleridge had gone to Bristol looking for the travelling chests he had sent on from his German expedition, and intended, if he failed to find them there, to continue his search in London. The chests unexpectedly arrived at Stowey only two days after his departure, but Sara's hopes that her husband would also reappear were disappointed. For several weeks they seem to have lost contact altogether, and in early November Sara shut up the cottage and took Hartley on a

The Lime Street cottage in the 1880s, when it had become 'Moore's Coleridge Cottage Inn'. By that time the cottage had been greatly enlarged and the roof raised

137

brief and necessary holiday to Old Cleeve, near Watchet, where they stayed with the Revd James Newton, a friend of Tom Poole's.[11]

Coleridge's disappearance was easily explained. After spending a few days in Bristol, during which he probably met the young Humphry Davy for the first time, he and Joseph Cottle travelled north to visit the Wordsworths in County Durham. Wordsworth and Dorothy had returned from Germany at the beginning of May, and since that time had been living with the Hutchinson family in the village of Sockburn-on-Tees. Mary Hutchinson was one of Dorothy's oldest friends, and the family's hospitable farmhouse was to shelter Dorothy and her brother, both now homeless, almost until the end of the year. Coleridge was reunited with his friends on about 26 October, and the following day, with Wordsworth and Cottle, set off on his first exploration of the Lake District. He was overwhelmed by the beauty he discovered, and wrote ecstatically to Dorothy to describe the sun setting behind the snow-covered mountains, and the majestic harmony of the landscape near Derwent Water. 'It was to me a vision of a fair Country,' he wrote. 'Why were you not with us Dorothy?'[12]

Coleridge carried his deep delight back to Sockburn in November, and shared it both with Dorothy and with the Hutchinsons, whom he now came to know better. Two members of the family, in particular, were destined to have central places in the lives of Coleridge and Wordsworth: in 1802, Mary Hutchinson accepted Wordsworth's proposal of marriage; and well before that time, her younger sister, Sarah, was becoming the object of Coleridge's passionate, tormented devotion. He mythologized her as 'Asra', and would repeatedly return to her in his writing and his thoughts for many years to come.

The claims on his attention of another Sara were more pressing that winter. At the beginning of December, he tried to contact his wife through Joseph Cottle, to relay the news that they were to 'reside in London for the next four months'. Soon afterwards he settled with Sara and Hartley in a house off the Strand, and until mid-February 1800 gave himself to the exhausting drudgery of writing for the *Morning Post*. He had no choice: 'The expences of my last year made it necessary for me to exert my industry.'[13] At the same time, he was searching for a house to replace the Lime Street cottage, the tenancy of which had finally been given up at Christmas 1799. 'I shall beyond all doubt settle at Stowey,' he wrote to Tom Poole in February, 'if I can get a suitable House – that is – a House with a Garden, & large enough for me to have a Study out of the noise of Women & children.' But none of the houses suggested by Poole seemed capable of satisfying Coleridge: Philip Hancock's old house was too near the centre of Stowey, and another house had a shared kitchen which was bound to be the cause of arguments. Coleridge would have been content with a cottage in Aisholt, a tiny and utterly remote Quantock village on his old route to Taunton. But 'Sara being Sara, and I being I, we must live in a town or else close to one, so that she may have neighbours and acquaintances.' As one suggestion after another was rejected, Coleridge's mind drifted from practical plans to day-dreams. He told

Derwent Water and
Skiddaw, 1808

Tom Poole in late February 1800 that he had a '*huge Hankering*' for Alfoxden, and
in the following month he was even trying to convince himself that Wordsworth
might take the house again. But that, he quickly realized, was impossible.
'. . . He will never quit the North of England,' Coleridge wrote to Tom Poole in
March; 'his habits are more assimilated with the Inhabitants there.'[14]

During a visit to Stowey in May and June, Coleridge still maintained, and half
believed, the fiction that he might return to Somerset, but in reality the decision
to settle near the Wordsworths in the Lake District had already been made, in
spite of Sara's 'mighty and numerous objections' to living at so great a distance
from her family and friends. At the end of June Coleridge was staying with the
Wordsworths in their new home at Grasmere, and devoted himself to the
preparation of a revised and expanded edition of the *Lyrical Ballads*. Finally, in the
last week of July, he and Sara settled fourteen miles away at Keswick, in part of a
spacious house called Greta Hall. Coleridge was listless and weak from 'a
rheumatic fever', and dosed himself with opium. But as he looked out from Greta
Hall to the lakes and mountains for which he had exchanged the landscape of his

Greta Hall and
Keswick Bridge,
c. 1830

native West Country, he hoped that he had entered now on a new period of creativity. Instead, there lay before him thirteen increasingly desperate years that almost brought him to destruction.[15]

Tom Poole bitterly regretted the decision to abandon Somerset, which he attributed, with an equal mixture of jealousy and justice, to Coleridge's uncritical 'prostration' before the stronger personality of Wordsworth. News from Keswick seemed to be only of illness, and Poole, as in the days when Coleridge was a neighbour, showered his friend with well-meant advice, urging in one letter the benefits of 'living by rule' and *appropriate* exercise'. He also added, with more than a hint of reproach, 'I fancy if you had continued here this would not have happened.' Coleridge himself felt the separation from Tom Poole and the Quantocks with unexpected force. 'My situation here is indeed a delightful situation,' he wrote to Josiah Wedgwood in November; 'but I feel what I have lost – feel it deeply – it recurs more often & more painfully, than I had anticipated.'[16]

Coleridge did not visit Stowey again until late December 1801, by which time both his health and his marriage appeared to be in their final decay. Travelling by way of London and Bath through violent storms, he arrived at Stowey just after Christmas, and for three weeks enjoyed the companionship not only of Poole, but also of Tom Wedgwood. Coleridge was in deep despair about his marriage, and wrote from Castle Street to Southey that his life was 'gangrened . . . in it's very vitals' by his loss of domestic happiness: '. . . I would gladly lie down by the side of the road, & become the Country for a mighty nation of Maggots.' But West Somerset, even in a frosty mid-winter, had something of its old effect on him, and by the end of his visit he felt himself 'exceedingly improved in health, spirits, & activity': Poole had evidently insisted on a regular diet and the avoidance of opium.[17]

Coleridge and Poole travelled back to London together, and there attended a lecture at the Royal Institution given by Humphry Davy, by now the trusted friend of both men. When they parted, Coleridge was in a mood of fragile optimism, and wrote to Sara of returning to her 'in Love & chearfulness, & therefore in pleasurable Convalescence, if not in Health'. But the optimistic moment was short-lived. When he visited the Wordsworths on a rainy afternoon in March, Dorothy was shocked and distressed at his appearance, thinking he seemed 'half stupefied'; and shortly afterwards, at Greta Hall, he wrote out his pain and grief to Sarah Hutchinson in a long verse-letter, soon brilliantly redrafted as 'Dejection: an Ode'.[18] 'Dejection' was one of the few undoubtedly great poems to be written by Coleridge in the years following his departure from Stowey. It examined his tortured sense that his 'shaping spirit of Imagination' lay dormant, and that the joy which had so animated him in his Stowey days had been crushed by a weight of troubles. The poem, written for the woman he now

Kilve Church and chantry in winter. Watercolour by W.W. Wheatley, 1847

141

loved with a desperate, unconsummated passion, was published on 4 October 1802, the same day on which Wordsworth was married to Mary Hutchinson, and the anniversary of Coleridge's own marriage seven years earlier in Bristol.

Visits to Tom Poole – 'a very, very good man' – and to the Wedgwood brothers at Tarrant Gunville in Dorset, occupied Coleridge during the early weeks of 1803.[19] In the company of these old and attentive friends, his health and spirits again seemed to improve; but the respite was as temporary as every other had been in a life now completely in the thrall of opium. For over two years, in Malta and Italy, he attempted to recover his health and to raise himself from despair and creative paralysis. But when, in 1807, he arrived at Stowey for what would prove to be his final visit, Coleridge had solved nothing in his personal or creative life. He was as hopelessly addicted to opium as he had ever been, as tortured by his love for Sarah Hutchinson, and as unable to produce anything that seemed worthy of his genius.

Memories of Stowey had been much in Coleridge's thoughts shortly before his last visit began in June 1807. In January, staying in Leicestershire with the Wordsworths, he had listened on successive evenings while Wordsworth read out the completed manuscript of *The Prelude*, the great autobiographical poem which he addressed to Coleridge.[20] In its closing pages the poem turned with loving recollection to the Alfoxden summer nine years earlier, when all had still seemed possible:

> That summer when on Quantock's grassy Hills
> Far ranging, and among the sylvan Coombs,
> Thou in delicious words, with happy heart,
> Didst speak the Vision of that Ancient Man,
> The bright-eyed Mariner, and rueful woes
> Didst utter of the Lady Christabel;
> And I, associate in such labour, walk'd
> Murmuring of him who, joyous hap! was found,
> After the perils of his moonlight ride
> Near the loud Waterfall; or her who sate
> In misery near the miserable Thorn . . .

The Prelude, so clearly an achievement of extraordinary range and power, was a reminder to Coleridge both of the central relationship of his life, and of his own failed creativity, and must have returned to him constantly as he explored for one last time the scenes of his greatest happiness.

He had travelled west intending to visit his brother George in Ottery, and had brought with him Sara and their children (Hartley, now aged ten, had gained a

Tom Poole's house in St Mary's Street, Nether Stowey

Tom Poole's bookroom. In the corner is the alcove which contained a bed

All Saints' Church,
Aisholt,
photographed *c.* 19

brother Derwent in 1800, and a sister Sara two years later). But when George heard that Coleridge had now firmly decided on a permanent separation from his wife, he refused to receive them, and the Stowey visit, intended to last for two weeks, was eventually prolonged to more than twelve.[21]

Coleridge and Sara were given a memorable welcome by Tom Poole, who had by now let his Castle Street home to Thomas Ward, and was comfortably established in a fine, large house in St Mary's Street. 'The children talk for evermore of the happiness of Stowey,' Sara wrote to Tom Poole later in the year, and for Coleridge, too, these Stowey weeks marked a period of deepening content, as well as of improving health. He sat and read in Poole's splendid, airy bookroom, which even contained a hidden alcove with a bed where he could sleep; he spent long hours talking in the old familiar way, and impressed his host with a mind whose '*great* qualities' were now better disciplined, and whose information was 'much extended'; he watched one day as the Stowey Women's Friendly Society, founded by Tom Poole, processed down St Mary's Street to the church; and in the company of Poole he went for miles in fine summer weather, retracing the 'dear old walks, of Quantock & Alfoxden'. Poole's only deficiency as a walking companion, Coleridge decided, was his incorrigible tendency to meander, which meant that a walk from Stowey to Enmore (where John Poole now lived) was quite likely to take in Fairfield, Periton, and Combwich as well.[22]

Enmore Castle, 1783. The building was largely demolished in 1834

Often Coleridge explored alone, and almost by accident one afternoon he took the road from Plainsfield to Aisholt, where he paid a final visit to his old friend John Brice, the rector. After dinner at the rectory Coleridge reminisced over a bottle of port about John Cruikshank, and then followed the darkening lanes back to Stowey. On another occasion he visited Lord Egmont at Enmore Castle – a vast eighteenth-century folly, complete with a moat – where he walked in the park among the great burr-oaks, and delighted Lord Egmont by talking 'very much like an angel'.[23]

It was during his absence at Enmore Castle that a young man came searching for him at Tom Poole's house. Thomas De Quincey, then twenty-two years old, had heard in Bristol that Coleridge was visiting the West Country, and was determined that the man he had long known through his work – especially 'The

Ancient Mariner' – should now be sought out in person.[24] Poole invited De Quincey to stay with him at Stowey until Coleridge returned, and had soon startled his young guest, who had taken Poole for a 'plain-looking farmer', by the breadth of his knowledge and the magnificence of his library. Days passed, but Coleridge did not appear, and it was finally Lord Egmont himself who brought news that his visitor had gone on from Enmore to Bridgwater.

De Quincey eventually found Coleridge standing under a gateway at the home of his Bridgwater friend John Chubb. He was in a deep reverie, and only some time after De Quincey first spoke did Coleridge return to 'day-light realities'. He welcomed his unknown disciple with kindness, and strolled with him through the Bridgwater streets in the warmth of a summer evening, while the people of the town stopped to enquire about Coleridge's health, and to urge him to make 'a lengthened stay' among them. 'Rarely, perhaps never,' De Quincey remembered, 'have I seen a person so much interrupted in one hour's space as Coleridge, on this occasion, by the courteous attentions of young and old.'

A much more remarkable spectacle awaited De Quincey at a large dinner party held on the same day at John Chubb's house. It was there that Coleridge embarked, as he was no doubt expected to do, on a 'continuous strain of eloquent dissertation' which seemed to De Quincey 'like some great river, the Orellana, or

Entrance to Bridgwater in th late eighteenth century. Lithogr after a drawing John Chubb

the St Lawrence'. Coleridge's theme was Hartleian philosophy, and for three hours he talked almost uninterruptedly, delivering 'many most striking aphorisms, embalming more weight of truth, and separately more deserving to be themselves embalmed than any that are on record'. De Quincey parted from Coleridge at about ten o'clock, and decided to make his way back to Bristol in the cool of the night, since his racing mind would not let him sleep. As he rode on past the dying fires of a village fair and through a landscape 'divinely calm', he was already forming the opinion he would later record: that the sad, opium-blighted man he had just left at Bridgwater possessed 'the largest and most spacious intellect, the subtlest and the most comprehensive . . . that has yet existed amongst men'.

Before Coleridge left Stowey in September, his thoughts had turned once more to plans for settling near Tom Poole. He visited an empty house, at Kingston St Mary, and paced out the rooms – a parlour, '6 by 4 Strides', a hall, '4½ broad, 6½ long', and several large bedrooms. He walked round a garden filled with fruit trees, and looked out on a magnificent prospect of the Vale of Taunton.[25] But it was only another day-dream. His tortured nights were more nearly the reality of his life: on 13 September he woke in the early morning at Tom Poole's house and recorded in his notebook his anguished love for Sarah Hutchinson.[26] In another notebook entry he wrote:

All the realities about me lose their natural *healing* powers, at least, diminish the same, & become not worthy of a Thought. . . . Pain is easily subdued compared with continual uncomfortableness – and the sense of stifled Power! . . . Die, my Soul, die! – Suicide – rather than this, the worst state of Degradation![27]

In the years that followed Coleridge's last Stowey visit he established a brilliant reputation as a lecturer, and resumed the 'periodical industry' of his *Watchman* days by establishing a weekly paper called *The Friend*. He lived much with the Wordsworths, until a quarrel in 1810, only ever imperfectly resolved, undermined their friendship; and all the time, his opium addiction was leading him inevitably towards a decisive breakdown. It came during the winter of 1813, when he had returned once more to the West Country to give two series of lectures in Bristol. Between late October and late November he lectured on Shakespeare and Milton, and was intending to begin a further series in the city on 7 December.[28] But the lectures never took place. Reaching Bath on 2 December, Coleridge broke his journey to Bristol by lodging at The Greyhound, in Bath's busy High Street; and it was there that a physical and mental crisis, induced by opium and alcohol, finally overcame him. For seven tormented days, he endured terrible suffering, and was 'forced to struggle and struggle' to keep himself from

High Street, Bath
looking towards
abbey, 1829. The
Greyhound Inn w
among the buildi
on the right-hand
side of the street

suicide. He scarcely slept, and was racked by extreme pain; 'yet the anguish & remorse of Mind was worse than the pain of the whole Body'. Only through the devoted care of Dr Parry, a Bath physician, did he survive the crisis, emerging from it with a clear sense that he must either begin to curb his addiction, or be destroyed by it.[29]

His old friend, Josiah Wade, took him into his home in Bristol, where, at Coleridge's own request, an attendant was employed to prevent him from obtaining opium. He tricked and lied his way to further supplies of the drug on numerous occasions, but the slow and erratic progress to partial rehabilitation had at last begun. At the end of the year Coleridge found shelter with his friends John and Mary Morgan at Calne in Wiltshire, and it was there in 1815 that he dictated to Morgan the *Biographia Literaria*, a brilliant and discursive work of autobiography, literary criticism and philosophy, which was published two years later.[30]

Calne, Wiltshire,
from the canal,
c. 1830

The stable and secure existence he had sought for so long – perhaps ever since his departure from Ottery as a child – was discovered finally in the home of James Gillman, a Highgate surgeon. Coleridge first lived with Gillman and his wife as a temporary patient; but his stay with them had soon been indefinitely extended, and from 1816, when he was forty-three years old, until his death eighteen years later, Coleridge was to remain their permanent house-guest and dear friend. In his room at the top of the Gillmans' house he read, wrote and received visitors, 'like a sage escaped from the inanity of life's battle'. Sara and his children saw him there occasionally, and Tom Poole also called, meeting his old friend for the last time in May 1834. Coleridge's mind, although as strong as ever, seemed to Poole 'impatient to take leave of its encumbrance', and two months later, on 25 July 1834, the end came. Coleridge was sixty-one years old, and was buried in Highgate churchyard, an exile to the last.[31]

Southey's response to the news of Coleridge's death was a mean-spirited recital of old grievances. But Wordsworth immediately forgot that any shadow had ever fallen over their relationship, remembering only the '*wonderful* man' who had leapt the gate at Racedown almost forty years earlier. Perhaps no one mourned more deeply than Charles Lamb, who had first known Coleridge as a bewildered Devonshire schoolboy. 'His great and dear spirit haunts me,' Lamb wrote; 'never saw I his likeness, nor probably the world can see again. I seem to love the house he died in more passionately than when he lived. What was his mansion is consecrated to me a chapel.'[32]

☆

Samuel Taylor
Coleridge in 1814.
Portrait by
Washington Allsto
a copy of which
hung over the
mantelpiece in To
Poole's bookroom

For those who had known Coleridge in his hopeful youth the West Country would always seem haunted by his presence. Southey, on leaving Bristol in 1803, had vowed never to return to a city so filled with ambivalent memories, but in the winter of 1836, two years after Coleridge's death, he was drawn back on a farewell visit to the settings in which the course of his life had largely been determined. He stayed in Bristol with Joseph Cottle, and there read the manuscript of Cottle's *Early Recollections of Coleridge and Southey*, a book whose appearance in 1837 was to cause much distress to the Ottery Coleridges; he revisited Bedminster, the home of his grandparents; and he saw once more the little house in College Street where the delusion of Pantisocratic brotherhood had finally been dispelled.[33]

Tom Poole welcomed Southey at Nether Stowey in December, and travelled on with him as far as Holnicote, near Porlock, before the two men parted for the last time. 'How like a dream does the past appear,' Southey wrote to Joseph Cottle that year; and soon even the dream was gone. Southey's mind began to fail, and when Wordsworth visited in 1840, Southey was unable to recognize him. Wordsworth thought at first that some 'slight glimpse of remembrance' crossed Southey's mind when they met, but a moment later the old man walked silently into his library, and taking down a book from the shelf, mechanically

Tom Poole in old age

turned its pages 'without reading, or the power of reading'. He died in the spring of 1843.[34]

Wordsworth's farewell visit to the West Country, in April and May 1841, was undertaken with a much deeper and more forgiving affection for Coleridge than Southey had ever possessed. His immediate reason for travelling west was to attend the marriage of his daughter Dora to Edward Quillinan, an old friend of the family. The ceremony took place at St James's Church, Bath, on 11 May, and next day William and Mary Wordsworth, their son Willy, the Quillinans, and Isabella Fenwick – the dear friend of Wordsworth's later years – moved on to Wells, where they stayed the night. They had breakfast the following morning at

Tom Poole's memorial in Nether Stowey Church

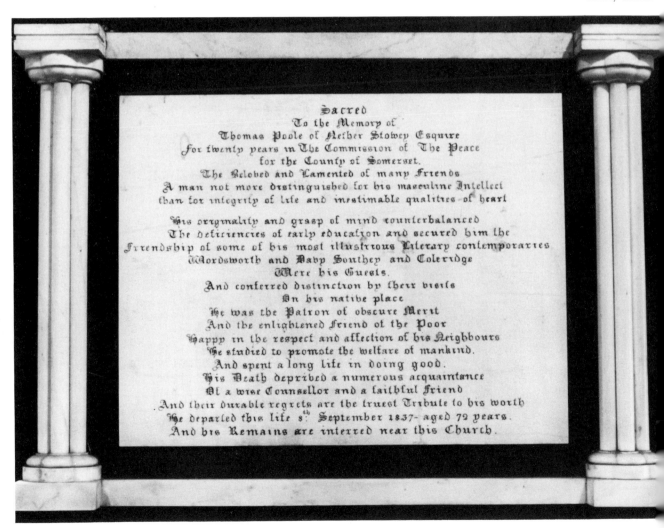

Piper's Inn, on the coach road a few miles from Glastonbury, and then entered the territory beyond Bridgwater that Wordsworth had last seen almost forty-three years earlier. Even in the company of his wife and family, Wordsworth's thoughts must have turned, most of all, to those who were absent that day: Dorothy had for several years been sunk in premature senility; Coleridge was seven years gone; and even Tom Poole was dead. He had died in September 1837, aged seventy-two, and now lay beneath a great ledger stone in the churchyard at Stowey.[35]

Wordsworth regretted the changes he found in the village of Holford; but at Alfoxden the passing years had made little difference, and the familiar scenes released from him a flood of recollection. From the house, where he was welcomed by Mr St Albyn, he looked out to the familiar larch tree, commemorated so long ago in the poem he had written for Dorothy; he took his family to the park gate and pointed to the place where Christopher Tricky's hovel had stood; and in Holford Glen, the 'chosen resort' in which he had composed 'Lines Written in Early Spring', he stood once more at the 'loud Waterfall', which had roared on during all the years of his absence. He was, Isabella Fenwick wrote, 'delighted to see again those scenes . . . where he had felt and thought so much.'[36]

For a few days after the Alfoxden visit the Wordsworths stayed in the Quantocks at Bagborough House, the home of Miss Fenwick's sister, Susan Popham. Then they set off on the road to Ottery St Mary to perform one final act

Bagborough House, where Wordsworth stayed during his West Country journey of 1841

of homage to the past. Although Wordsworth had never visited Ottery, the visionary intensity with which Coleridge had so often described the town made it an almost familiar place. No doubt Wordsworth saw the schoolmaster's house, where Coleridge had been born, and the long, low schoolroom where his father had presided. Certainly he visited St Mary's Church, and it was there, by chance, that he met Coleridge's nephew, Francis George Coleridge, who invited him to take tea at the Manor House before his visit came to an end.[37]

☆

Wordsworth lived much with thoughts of the past in his old age. He began to rediscover and revise manuscripts of his early work, and published some of it, including *The Borderers*, in a volume of 1842 called *Poems, Chiefly of Early and Late Years*. To Isabella Fenwick he dictated his memories of the circumstances which had given rise to many of his poems, among them the poems of the Alfoxden year. And always, as a painful reminder of happier times, he had before him the sight of his stricken sister, and also of Hartley Coleridge, who lived near by. Hartley – 'the poet-child of a poet-father' – had grown up possessing much of his father's ability, and many of his weaknesses. He was plagued by the same infirmity of will, as well as by bouts of remorseful self-accusation, and forfeited a promising career as an Oxford fellow through his persistent drunkenness. From 1822 he lived mostly in the Lake District, where he would disappear for days at a time to wander the mountains and lake shores, the very scenes Coleridge had wished for him in 'Frost at Midnight'. He was greatly loved by the local people for his kindness and simplicity of manner, and was watched over by Wordsworth with a fatherly concern. When Hartley died in 1849, at the age of only fifty-two, Wordsworth was much affected, remembering the little child in the cottage at Stowey whom Coleridge had loved with such a powerful devotion. Wordsworth managed only a few sad words on hearing the news, but then, thinking of the place in Grasmere churchyard he had chosen for Mary and himself, he said, 'Let him lie by us – he would have wished it.'[38]

Fifteen months later, in April 1850, Wordsworth was buried close to Hartley, and in the new year of 1855, Dorothy joined them, released finally from her long mental dissolution. Mary survived for four more years, until in 1859 she became the last of her generation to be carried to the angle of the churchyard where the Wordsworths lie. The stream that feeds Grasmere lake flows near their graves, and all around, the mountains rise up.

☆

am Wordsworth
d age. After a
ait by
Pickersgill,

Almost at once, literary pilgrims began to visit the West Country to discover the settings in which Coleridge and Wordsworth had lived and worked. As early as 1839, a correspondent to the *Bristol Journal* was writing to identify the Clevedon

Grasmere Church,
where the
Wordsworths and
Hartley Coleridge
are buried

cottage in which Coleridge and Sara had spent their early married life, and others
came searching for the few survivors who could still remember Tom Poole and
his friends. The Revd John Poole, in mid-century, was happy to recall for curious
visitors those occasions at his cousin Tom's house, almost a lifetime earlier, when
Coleridge had talked 'sad democratic nonsense'; and Mr St Albyn, most
unpoetical of men, would retell his childhood memories of seeing Wordsworth
'mooning about the hills'.[39] But genuine traditions were few, and the complex
geography of the Quantock Hills, together with a general absence of identifiable

landscape detail in the poems and letters, prevented West Somerset from becoming a literary shrine comparable to the Lakes.

And yet much that was familiar to Coleridge and the Wordsworths has survived recognizably almost two centuries after their departure. The gloomy cottage where Sara watched with her dying child still stands at the entrance to Stowey, and Tom Poole's fine house has continued to dominate Castle Street. Near Holford and Alfoxden, most of all, change has come slowly. The brook flows down from Holford Combe just as it did when Coleridge and the Wordsworths would trace it to the sea at Kilve; Alfoxden remains elegant and alone in the midst of the Alfoxden deer park; and the wooded lane to the mansion – surely one of the most evocative places among the literary landscapes of England – can hardly have changed since the spring day in 1798 when Coleridge 'talked far above singing' to the young William Hazlitt.

Above all, the Quantocks themselves remain, rising abruptly from a pattern of Somerset fields. Seen from Higher Hare Knap or from Dowsborough, the bracken-covered hills can still achieve the startling beauty to which Coleridge and the Wordsworths responded with such power, and which lay near the heart of those Quantock years of poetry and of friendship.

DOROTHY WORDSWORTH'S ALFOXDEN JOURNAL, 1798[1]

ALFOXDEN, *January 20th* 1798. – The green paths down the hill-sides are channels for streams. The young wheat is streaked by silver lines of water running between the ridges, the sheep are gathered together on the slopes. After the wet dark days, the country seems more populous. It peoples itself in the sunbeams. The garden, mimic of spring, is gay with flowers. The purple-starred hepatica spreads itself in the sun, and the clustering snow-drops put forth their white heads, at first upright, ribbed with green, and like a rosebud;[2] when completely opened, hanging their heads downwards, but slowly lengthening their slender stems. The slanting woods of an unvarying brown, showing the light through the thin net-work of their upper boughs. Upon the highest ridge of that round hill covered with planted oaks, the shafts of the trees show in the light like the columns of a ruin.

21st. – Walked on the hill-tops – a warm day. Sate under the firs in the park. The tops of the beeches of a brown-red or crimson. Those oaks fanned by the sea breeze thick with feathery sea-green moss, as a grove not stripped of its leaves. Moss cups more proper than acorns for fairy goblets.

22nd. – Walked through the wood to Holford.[3] The ivy twisting round the oaks like bristled serpents. The day cold – a warm shelter in the hollies, capriciously bearing berries. Query: Are the male and female flowers on separate trees?

23rd. – Bright sunshine, went out at 3 o'clock. The sea perfectly calm blue, streaked with deeper colour by the clouds, and tongues or points of sand; on our return of a gloomy red. The sun gone down. The crescent moon, Jupiter, and Venus. The sound of the sea distinctly heard on the tops of the hills, which we could never hear in summer. We attribute this partly to the bareness of the trees, but chiefly to the absence of the singing of birds, the hum of insects, that noiseless noise which lives in the summer air. The villages marked out by beautiful beds of smoke. The turf fading into the mountain road. The scarlet flowers of the moss.

24th. – Walked between half-past three and half-past five. The evening cold and clear. The sea of a sober grey, streaked by the deeper grey clouds. The half dead sound of the near sheep-bell, in the hollow of the sloping coombe, exquisitely soothing.

25th. – Went to Poole's after tea. The sky spread over with one continuous cloud, whitened by the light of the moon, which, though her dim shape was seen, did not throw forth so strong a light as to chequer the earth with shadows. At once the clouds seemed to cleave asunder, and left her in the centre of a black-blue vault. She sailed along, followed by multitudes of stars, small, and bright, and sharp. Their brightness seemed concentrated, (half-moon).

26th. – Walked upon the hill-tops; followed the sheep tracks till we overlooked the larger coombe.[4] Sat in the sunshine. The distant sheep-bells, the sound of the stream; the woodman winding along the half-marked road with his laden pony; locks of wool still spangled with the dewdrops; the blue-grey sea shaded with immense masses of cloud, not streaked; the sheep glittering in the sunshine. Returned through the wood. The trees skirting the wood, being exposed more directly to the action of the sea breeze, stripped of the net-work of their upper boughs, which are stiff and erect, like black skeletons; the ground strewed with the red berries of the holly. Set forward before two o'clock. Returned a little after four.

27th. – Walked from seven o'clock till half-past eight. Upon the whole an uninteresting evening. Only once while we were in the wood the moon burst through the invisible veil which enveloped her, the shadows of the oaks blackened, and their lines became more strongly marked. The withered leaves were coloured with a deeper yellow, a brighter gloss spotted the hollies; again her form became dimmer; the sky flat, unmarked by distances, a white thin cloud. The manufacturer's dog makes a strange, uncouth howl, which it continues many minutes after there is no noise near it but that of the brook. It howls at the murmur of the village stream.[5]

28th. – Walked only to the mill.[6]

29th. – A very stormy day. William walked to the top of the hill to see the sea. Nothing distinguishable but a heavy blackness. An immense bough riven from one of the fir trees.

30th. – William called me into the garden to observe a singular appearance about the moon. A perfect rainbow, within the bow one star, only of colours more vivid. The semi-circle soon became a complete circle, and in the course of three or four minutes the whole faded away. Walked to the blacksmith's and the baker's; an uninteresting evening.

31st. – Set forward to Stowey at half-past five. A violent storm in the wood; sheltered under the hollies.[7] When we left home the moon immensely large, the sky scattered over with clouds. These soon closed in, contracting the dimensions of the moon without concealing her. The sound of the pattering shower, and the gusts of wind, very grand. Left the wood when nothing remained of the storm but the driving wind, and a few scattering drops of rain. Presently all clear, Venus first showing herself between the struggling clouds; afterwards Jupiter appeared. The hawthorn hedges black and pointed, glittering with millions of diamond drops; the hollies shining with broader patches of light. The road to the village of Holford glittered like another stream. On our return, the wind high – a violent storm of hail and rain at the Castle of Comfort.[8] All the Heavens seemed in one perpetual motion when the rain ceased; the moon appearing, now half veiled, and now retired behind heavy clouds, the stars still moving, the roads very dirty.

February 1st. – About two hours before dinner, set forward towards Mr Bartelmy's.[9] The wind blew so keen in our faces that we felt ourselves inclined to seek the covert of the wood. There we had a warm shelter, gathered a burthen of large rotten boughs blown down by the wind of the preceding night. The sun shone clear, but all at once a heavy blackness hung over the sea. The trees almost *roared*, and the ground seemed in motion with the multitudes of dancing leaves, which made a rustling sound distinct from that of the trees. Still the asses pastured in quietness under the hollies, undisturbed by these forerunners of the storm. The wind beat furiously against us as we returned. Full moon. She rose in uncommon majesty over the sea, slowly ascending through the clouds. Sat with the window open an hour in the moonlight.

2nd. – Walked through the wood, and on to the Downs before dinner; a warm pleasant air. The sun shone, but was often obscured by straggling clouds. The redbreasts made a ceaseless song in the woods. The wind rose very high in the evening. The room smoked so that we were obliged to quit it. Young lambs in a green pasture in the Coombe, thick legs, large heads, black staring eyes, gaunt as a new-dropped lamb.[10]

3rd. – A mild morning, the windows open at breakfast, the redbreasts singing in the garden. Walked with Coleridge over the hills.[11] The sea at first obscured by vapour; that vapour afterwards slid in one mighty mass along the sea-shore; the islands[12] and one point of land clear beyond it. The distant country (which was purple in the clear dull air), overhung by straggling clouds that sailed over it, appeared like the darker clouds, which are often seen at a great distance apparently motionless, while the nearer ones pass quickly over them, driven by the lower winds. I never saw such a union of earth, sky, and sea. The clouds beneath our feet spread themselves to the water, and the clouds of the sky almost joined them. Gathered sticks in the wood; a perfect stillness. The redbreasts sang upon the leafless boughs. Of a great number of sheep in the field, only one standing. Returned to dinner at five o'clock. The moonlight still and warm as a summer's night at nine o'clock.

4th. – Walked a great part of the way to Stowey with Coleridge. The morning warm and sunny. The young lasses seen on the hill-tops, in the villages and roads, in their summer holiday clothes – pink petticoats and blue. Mothers with their children in arms, and the little ones that could just walk, tottering by their side. Midges or small flies spinning in the sunshine; the songs of the lark and redbreast; daisies upon the turf; the hazels in blossom; honeysuckles budding. I saw one solitary strawberry flower under a hedge. The furze gay with blossom. The moss rubbed from the pailings by the sheep, that leave locks of wool, and the red marks with which they are spotted, upon the wood.

5th. – Walked to Stowey with Coleridge, returned by Woodlands;[13] a very warm day. In the continued singing of birds distinguished the notes of a blackbird or thrush. The sea overshadowed by a thick dark mist, the land in sunshine. The sheltered oaks and beeches still retaining their brown leaves. Observed some trees putting out red shoots. Query: What trees are they?[14]

6th. – Walked to Stowey over the hills, returned to tea, a cold and clear evening, the roads in some parts frozen hard. The sea hid by mist all the day.

7th. – Turned towards Potsdam,[15] but finding the way dirty, changed our course. Cottage gardens the object of our walk. Went up the smaller Coombe to Woodlands, to the blacksmith's, the baker's, and through the village of Holford. Still misty over the sea. The air very delightful. We saw nothing very new, or interesting.

8th. – Went up the Park, and over the tops of the hills, till we came to a new and very delicious pathway, which conducted us to the Coombe. Sat a considerable time upon the heath. Its surface restless and glittering with the motion of the scattered piles of withered grass, and the waving of the spiders' threads. On our return the mist still hanging over the sea, but the opposite coast clear, and the rocky cliffs distinguishable. In the deep Coombe, as we stood upon the sunless hill, we saw miles of grass, light and glittering, and the insects passing.

9th. – William gathered sticks. . . .[16]

10th. – Walked to Woodlands, and to the waterfall.[17] The adders-tongue and the ferns green in the low damp dell. These plants now in perpetual motion from the current of the air; in summer only moved by the drippings of the rocks. A cloudy day.

11th. – Walked with Coleridge near to Stowey. The day pleasant, but cloudy.

12th. – Walked alone to Stowey. Returned in the evening with Coleridge. A mild, pleasant, cloudy day.

13th. – Walked with Coleridge through the wood. A mild and pleasant morning, the near prospect clear. The ridges of the hills fringed with wood, showing the sea through them like the white sky, and still beyond the dim horizon of the distant hills, hanging as it were in one undetermined line between sea and sky.

14th. – Gathered sticks with William in the wood, he being unwell and not able to go further. The young birch trees of a bright red, through which gleams a shade of purple. Sat down in a thick part of the wood. The near trees still, even to their top-most boughs, but a perpetual motion in those that skirt the wood. The breeze rose gently; its path distinctly marked till it came to the very spot where we were.

15th. – Gathered sticks in the further wood. The dell[18] green with moss and brambles, and the tall and slender pillars of the unbranching oaks. I crossed the water with letters; returned to Wm. and Basil.[19] A shower met us in the wood, and a ruffling breeze.

16th. – Went for eggs into the Coombe, and to the baker's; a hail shower; brought home large burthens of sticks, a starlight evening, the sky closed in, and the ground white with snow before we went to bed.

17th. – A deep snow upon the ground. Wm. and Coleridge walked to Mr Bartelmy's, and to Stowey. Wm. returned, and we walked through the wood into the Coombe to fetch some eggs. The sun shone bright and clear. A deep stillness in the thickest part of the wood, undisturbed except by the occasional dropping of the snow from the holly boughs; no other sound but that of the water, and the slender notes of a redbreast, which sang at intervals on the outskirts of the southern side of the wood. There the bright green moss was bare at the roots of the trees, and the little birds were upon it. The whole appearance of the wood was enchanting; and each tree, taken singly, was beautiful. The branches of the hollies pendent with their white burden, but still showing their bright red berries, and their glossy green leaves. The bare branches of the oaks thickened by the snow.

18th. – Walked after dinner beyond Woodlands. A sharp and very cold evening; first observed the crescent moon, a silvery line, a thready bow, attended by Jupiter and Venus in their palest hues.

19th. – I walked to Stowey before dinner; Wm. unable to go all the way. Returned alone; a fine sunny, clear, frosty day. The sea still, and blue, and broad, and smooth.

20th. – Walked after dinner towards Woodlands.

21st. – Coleridge came in the morning, which prevented our walking. Wm. went through the wood with him towards Stowey; a very stormy night.

22nd. – Coleridge came in the morning to dinner. Wm. and I walked after dinner to Woodlands; the moon and two planets; sharp and frosty. Met a razor-grinder with a soldier's jacket on, a knapsack upon his back, and a boy to drag his wheel. The sea very black, and making a loud noise as we came through the wood, loud as if disturbed, and the wind was silent.

23rd. – William walked with Coleridge in the morning. I did not go out.

24th. – Went to the hill-top. Sat a considerable time overlooking the country towards the sea. The air blew pleasantly round us. The landscape mildly interesting. The Welsh hills capped by a huge range of tumultuous white clouds. The sea, spotted with white, of a bluish grey in general, and streaked with darker lines. The near shores clear; scattered farm houses, half-concealed by green mossy orchards, fresh straw lying at the doors; hay-stacks in the fields. Brown fallows, the springing wheat, like a shade of green over the brown earth, and the choice meadow plots, full of sheep and lambs, of a soft and vivid green; a few wreaths of blue smoke, spreading along the ground; the oaks and beeches in the hedges retaining their yellow leaves; the distant prospect on the land side, islanded with sunshine; the sea, like a basin full to the margin; the dark fresh-ploughed fields;[20] the turnips of a lively rough green. Returned through the wood.

25th. – I lay down in the morning, though the whole day was very pleasant, and the evening fine. We did not walk.

26th. – Coleridge came in the morning, and Mr and Mrs Cruikshank;[21] walked with the Coleridge nearly to Stowey after dinner. A very clear afternoon. We lay sidelong upon the turf, and gazed on the landscape till it melted into more than natural loveliness. The sea very uniform, of a pale greyish blue, only one distant bay, bright and blue as a sky; had there been a vessel sailing up it, a perfect image of delight. Walked to the top of a high hill to see a fortification.[22] Again sat down to feed upon the prospect; a magnificent scene, *curiously* spread out for even minute inspection, though so extensive that the mind is afraid to calculate its bounds. A winter prospect shows every cottage, every farm, and the forms of distant trees, such as in summer have no distinguishing mark. On our return, Jupiter and Venus before us. While the twilight still overpowered the light of the moon, we were reminded that she was shining bright above our heads, by our faint shadows going before us. We had seen her on the tops of the hills, melting into the blue sky. Poole called while we were absent.

27th. – I walked to Stowey in the evening. Wm. and Basil went with me through the wood. The prospect bright, yet *mildly* beautiful. The sea big and white, swelled to the very shores, but round and high in the middle. Coleridge returned with me, as far as the wood. A very bright moonlight night. Venus almost like another moon. Lost to us at Alfoxden long before she goes down the large white sea.

. . . . . .[23]

March 1st. – We rose early. A thick fog obscured the distant prospect entirely, but the shapes of the nearer trees and the dome of the wood dimly seen and dilated. It cleared away between ten and eleven. The shapes of the mist, slowly moving along, exquisitely beautiful; passing over the sheep they almost seemed to have more of life than those quiet creatures. The unseen birds singing in the mist.

2nd. – Went a part of the way home with Coleridge in the morning. Gathered fir apples afterwards under the trees.

3rd. – I went to the shoemaker's. William lay under the trees till my return. Afterwards went to the secluded farm house in search of eggs, and returned over the hill. A very mild, cloudy evening. The rose trees in the hedges and the elders budding.

4th. – Walked to Woodlands after dinner, a pleasant evening.

5th. – Gathered fir apples. A thick fog came on. Walked to the baker's and the shoemaker's, and through the fields towards Woodlands. On our return, found Tom Poole in the parlour. He drank tea with us.

6th. – A pleasant morning, the sea white and bright, and full to the brim. I walked to see Coleridge in the evening. William went with me to the wood. Coleridge very ill. It was a mild, pleasant afternoon, but the evening became very foggy; when I was near Woodlands, the fog overhead became thin, and I saw the shapes of the Central Stars. Again it closed, and the whole sky was the same.

7th. – William and I drank tea at Coleridge's. A cloudy sky. Observed nothing particularly interesting – the distant prospect obscured. One only leaf upon the top of a tree – the sole remaining leaf – danced round and round like a rag blown by the wind.[24]

8th. – Walked in the Park in the morning. I sate under the fir trees. Coleridge came after dinner, so we did not walk again. A foggy morning, but a clear sunny day.

9th. – A clear sunny morning, went to meet Mr. and Mrs. Coleridge. The day very warm.

10th. – Coleridge, Wm., and I walked in the evening to the top of the hill. We all passed the morning in sauntering about the park and gardens, the children playing about, the old man at the top of the hill gathering furze;[25] interesting groups of human creatures, the young frisking and dancing in the sun, the elder quietly drinking in the life and soul of the sun and air.

11th. – A cold day. The children went down towards the sea. William and I walked to the top of the hills above Holford. Met the blacksmith. Pleasant to see the labourer on Sunday jump with the friskiness of a cow upon a sunny day.

12th. – Tom Poole returned with Coleridge to dinner, a brisk, cold, sunny day; did not walk.

13th. – Poole dined with us. William and I strolled into the wood. Coleridge called us into the house.

. . . . . .

15th. – I have neglected to set down the occurrences of this week, so I do not recollect how we disposed of ourselves to-day.

16th. – William, and Coleridge, and I walked in the Park a short time. I wrote to ——.[26] William very ill, better in the evening; and we called round by Potsdam.

17th. – I do not remember this day.

18th. –The Coleridges left us. A cold, windy morning. Walked with them half way. On our return, sheltered under the hollies during a hail-shower. The withered leaves danced with the hailstones. William wrote a description of the storm.[27]

19th. – Wm. and Basil and I walked to the hill-tops, a very cold bleak day. We were met on our return by a severe hailstorm. William wrote some lines describing a stunted thorn.[28]

20th. – Coleridge dined with us. We went more than half way home with him in the evening. A very cold evening, but clear. The spring seemingly very little advanced. No green trees, only the hedges are budding, and looking very lovely.

21st. – We drank tea at Coleridge's. A quiet shower of snow was in the air during more than half our walk. At our return the sky partially shaded with clouds. The horned moon was set. Startled two night birds from the great elm tree.

22nd. – I spent the morning in starching and hanging out linen; walked *through* the wood in the evening, very cold.

23rd. – Coleridge dined with us. He brought his ballad finished.[29] We walked with him to the Miner's house.[30] A beautiful evening, very starry, the horned moon.

24th. – Coleridge, the Chesters,[31] and Ellen Crewkshank called. We walked with them through the wood. Went in the evening into the Coombe to get eggs; returned through the wood, and walked in the park. A duller night than last night: a sort of white shade over the blue sky. The stars dim. The spring continues to advance very slowly,[32] no green trees, the hedges leafless; nothing green but the brambles that still retain their old leaves, the evergreens, and the palms, which indeed are not absolutely green. Some brambles I observed to-day budding afresh, and those have shed their old leaves. The crooked arm of the old oak tree points upwards to the moon.

25th. – Walked to Coleridge's after tea. Arrived at home at one o'clock. The night cloudy but not dark.

26th. – Went to meet Wedgwood[33] at Coleridge's after dinner. Reached home at half-past twelve, a fine moonlight night; half moon.

27th. – Dined at Poole's. Arrived at home a little after twelve, a partially cloudy, but light night, very cold.

28th. – Hung out the linen.

29th. – Coleridge dined with us.

30th. – Walked I know not where.

31st. – Walked.

April 1st. – Walked by moonlight.[34]

2nd. – A very high wind. Coleridge came to avoid the smoke; stayed all night. We walked in the wood, and sat under the trees. The half of the wood perfectly still, while the wind was making a loud noise behind us. The still trees only gently bowed their heads, as if listening to the wind. The hollies in the thick wood unshaken by the blast; only, when it came with a greater force, shaken by the rain drops falling from the bare oaks above.

3rd. – Walked to Crookham, with Coleridge and Wm., to make the appeal.[35] Left Wm. there, and parted with Coleridge at the top of the hill. A very stormy afternoon. . . .

4th. – Walked to the sea-side in the afternoon. A great commotion in the air, but the sea neither grand nor beautiful. A violent shower in returning. Sheltered under some fir trees at Potsdam.

5th. – Coleridge came to dinner. William and I walked in the wood in the morning. I fetched eggs from the Coombe.

6th. – Went a part of the way home with Coleridge. A pleasant warm morning, but a showery day. Walked a short distance up the lesser Coombe, with an intention of going to the source of the brook, but the evening closing in, cold prevented us. The Spring still advancing very slowly. The horse-chestnuts budding, and the hedgerows beginning to look green, but nothing fully expanded.

7th. – Walked before dinner up the Coombe, to the source of the brook, and came home by the tops of the hills; a showery morning, at the hill-tops; the view opened upon us very grand.

8th. – Easter Sunday. Walked in the morning in the wood, and half way to Stowey; found the air at first oppressively warm, afterwards very pleasant.

9th. – Walked to Stowey, a fine air in going, but very hot in returning. The sloe in blossom, the hawthorns green, the larches in the park changed from black to green in two or three days. Met Coleridge in returning.

10th. – I was hanging out linen in the evening. We walked to Holford. I turned off to the baker's, and walked beyond Woodlands, expecting to meet William, met him on the hill; a close warm evening . . . in bloom.

11th. – In the wood in the morning, walked to the top of the hill, then I went down into the wood. A pleasant evening, a fine air, the grass in the park becoming green, many trees green in the dell.

12th. – Walked in the morning in the wood. In the evening up the Coombe, fine walk. The Spring advances rapidly, multitudes of primroses, dog-violets, periwinkles, stitchwort.

13th. – Walked in the wood in the morning. In the evening went to Stowey. I staid with Mr. Coleridge. Wm. went to Poole's. Supped with Mr Coleridge.[36]

14th. – Walked in the wood in the morning. The evening very stormy, so we staid within doors. Mary Wollstonecraft's life, etc., came.

15th. – Set forward after breakfast to Crookham, and returned to dinner at three o'clock. A fine cloudy morning. Walked about the squire's grounds. Quaint waterfalls about, about which Nature was very successfully striving to make beautiful what art had deformed – ruins, hermitages, &c., &c. In spite of all these things, the dell romantic and beautiful, though everywhere planted with unnaturalised trees.

Happily we cannot shape the huge hills, or carve out the valleys according to our fancy.[37]

16th. – New moon. William walked in the wood in the morning. I neglected to follow him. We walked in the park in the evening. . . .

17th. – Walked in the wood in the morning. In the evening upon the hill. Cowslips plentiful.

18th. – Walked in the wood, a fine sunny morning, met Coleridge returned from his brother's. He dined with us. We drank tea, and then walked with him nearly to Stowey. . . .

19th. – . . .

20th. – Walked in the evening up the hill[38] dividing the Coombes. Came home the Crookham way, by the thorn, and the little muddy pond. Nine o'clock at our return. William all the morning engaged in wearisome composition. The moon crescent. "Peter Bell" begun.

21st, 22nd, 23rd. – . . .

24th. – Walked a considerable time in the wood. Sat under the trees, in the evening walked on the top of the hill, found Coleridge on our return and walked with him towards Stowey.

25th. – Coleridge drank tea, walked with him to Stowey.

26th. – William went to have his picture taken.[39] I walked with him. Dined at home. Coleridge and he drank tea.

27th. – Coleridge breakfasted and drank tea, strolled in the wood in the morning, went with him in the evening through the wood, afterwards walked on the hills: the moon, a many-coloured sea and sky.

28th, Saturday. – A very fine morning, warm weather all the week.

May 6th, Sunday. – Expected the painter, and Coleridge. A rainy morning – very pleasant in the evening. Met Coleridge as we were walking out. Went with him to Stowey; heard the nightingale; saw a glow-worm.

7th. – Walked in the wood in the morning. In the evening, to Stowey with Coleridge who called.

8th. – Coleridge dined, went in the afternoon to tea at Stowey. A pleasant walk home.

9th. – . . . Wrote to Coleridge.

Wednesday, 16th May. – Coleridge, William, and myself set forward to the Chedder rocks; slept at Bridgewater.

22nd, Thursday.[40] – Walked to Chedder. Slept at Cross.[41]

Appendix II

GAZETTEER

Bath

Though they visited it infrequently, Bath had a significant place in the lives of both Coleridge and Wordsworth. Coleridge first entered the city in 1794 at the beginning of his earliest walking tour through Somerset. He stayed at 8 Westgate Buildings, the home of Southey's mother, and it was there, at the end of the tour, that Sara Fricker accepted his proposal of marriage. Westgate Buildings survive, though Mrs Southey's house has not been precisely identified. Almost twenty years later, in 1813, Coleridge reached the city on his way to lecture in Bristol. At the Greyhound Inn he succumbed to a mental and physical crisis which probably marked the lowest point of his life. The Greyhound stood on the west side of High Street near the junction with Upper Borough Walls. Modern buildings now occupy its site.

From 14 April to 11 May 1841 Wordsworth stayed at 9 North Parade, Bath. He was in the city for the wedding of his daughter Dora, the ceremony taking place at St James's Church (now destroyed) on 11 May. He attended Widcombe Church during his visit, and met his old friend Crabb Robinson, but on the day of the wedding was so overcome with emotion that he could not leave the house.

Bristol

The Second World War destroyed much of Bristol that was familiar to Coleridge and Wordsworth. Joseph Cottle's house in Wine Street, where Wordsworth probably wrote 'Tintern Abbey', has disappeared, as has Southey's birthplace, which stood nearby. At the junction of High Street and Corn Street, however, the building identified as Cottle's bookshop (49 High Street) still stands, though there must be some doubt that in its present form the building is the same that the poets visited so often. The Fricker family home on Redcliffe Hill, where Coleridge briefly lived, has vanished; but the Fricker's parish church, the magnificent St Mary Redcliffe, has escaped major change. Coleridge was married there in October 1795.

Near the cathedral and the council house is College Street, where, at no. 25 (not no. 48), Coleridge and Southey set up house early in 1795. College Street survives in name, but has lost most of its identity and all its older buildings. The town house of John Pretor Pinney is a short distance away at 7 Great George Street, and is open to the public as the Georgian House Museum. Pinney, a wealthy plantation owner, first occupied the newly-completed house in 1791, and in 1795 welcomed Wordsworth there as his guest. It is likely that some early meetings of Coleridge and Wordsworth took place at the house, though not, it seems, the very first. At the top of King Street stands the former City Library (now a restaurant) which Coleridge and Southey valued greatly and used often.

Ottery St Mary

Despite a disastrous fire in 1866 and expansion in the twentieth century, Ottery St Mary has retained its essential character as a small market town set in a landscape of great beauty. The schoolmaster's house where Coleridge was born and the schoolhouse where his father taught stood in the street called

The College immediately south of St Mary's Church. Both buildings were demolished in 1884, and a house called Grandisson Court now occupies their site. At the farther end of The College is the Warden's House, where old Mrs Coleridge took up residence following her husband's death in 1781, and which had earlier been the town residence of Sir Stafford Northcote, Coleridge's childhood rescuer. The Chanter's House, west of the church, is now largely the Victorian mansion Butterfield made in 1880–3, but also incorporates the earlier house where Coleridge visited his brother James in 1799. The Coleridge family never lived at the vicarage (properly called the Vicars' House).

Though nineteenth-century restorations considerably altered the internal appearance of St Mary's Church, it remains still an austerely beautiful example of fourteenth-century architecture. Coleridge's father is buried on the north side of the altar in an unmarked grave, his memorial stone, 'deep cut in Latin', having been removed to the Lady Chapel. Later Coleridges are commemorated in the south transept, which also contains Ottery's great medieval clock.

Just outside the town, at Cadhay Bridge, a footpath leads north beside the River Otter through the meadows which Coleridge knew so well. Another path follows the river southward, and after a mile reaches the sandstone cavern known as Pixies' Parlour. The initials 'STC', supposedly carved by the poet, can still be seen on the cavern wall.

Valley of the Rocks

The Valley of the Rocks, described by Hazlitt as 'bedded among precipices overhanging the sea', runs parallel to the North Devon coast immediately west of Lynmouth and Lynton. It probably marks the former course of the East Lyn River, but is now a dry valley bordered by towering rock formations eroded from the Devon sandstone. This desolate place was deeply impressive to Coleridge and the Wordsworths, who evidently walked the forty miles from Stowey to Lynton on many occasions, sometimes taking with them more or less willing companions such as Hazlitt and Cottle. Coleridge's prose tale, 'The Wanderings of Cain', draws inspiration directly from the setting of the valley.

DORSET

Racedown Lodge

Racedown Lodge, on the B3165 between Crewkerne and Lyme Regis, was built by John Pretor Pinney following his return from Nevis in 1783. His family had lived in West Dorset since at least the sixteenth century, and Racedown was intended by him as 'a lee-port in a storm', where he could escape the commercial pressures of Bristol.

William and Dorothy Wordsworth lived in the mansion rent-free from September 1795 until June 1797, Dorothy remembering it as the place 'dearest to my recollections upon the whole surface of the island'. She liked best of all the 'common parlour', describing it as 'the prettiest little room . . . with very neat furniture, a large book[case] on each side the fire, a marble chimney piece, bath stove, and an oil cloth for the floor'. The house has been altered and enlarged since the eighteenth century, but remains in many respects the building which the Wordsworths knew. The gateway at which Coleridge so dramatically appeared in June 1797 survives a short distance from the house, opposite Racedown Home Farm.

SOMERSET

Bridgwater

Bridgwater was a town Coleridge came to know well: it was the place which marked either the beginning or the end of many journeys by coach and carrier during his Somerset years, and was the only substantial town within immediate reach of Stowey.

Bridgwater was Somerset's leading port, and by the eighteenth century the ships which Coleridge saw along the quays by the River Parrett were taking Bridgwater's own bricks, tiles, and glass to distant markets. His friend, John Chubb, lived in a house (now gone) which stood on the south side of Fore Street near the bridge, and it was under a gateway to the house that Thomas De Quincey discovered Coleridge on a day in 1807. A short distance away, the Unitarian chapel still stands in

Dampiet Street. Coleridge often preached there for his friend John Howel, the minister; a plaque on the chapel wall records a few of his visits.

Clevedon

Clevedon was a small and scattered village when Coleridge and his wife reached it in 1795. By 1830 its mushroom growth as a seaside resort had already begun, and today Clevedon is a substantial and only intermittently attractive town. 'Myrtle Cottage' (55 Old Church Road) is usually identified as the house in which Coleridge spent his early married life, and stands on a busy, built-up road near the town centre. Its claims to have a connection with Coleridge are doubtful: Joseph Cottle said the cottage was 'in the western extremity, not in the centre of the village', a description more appropriate to a setting near the parish church, almost a mile from the town centre. Certain identification is now impossible.

Coleridge would recognize little at Clevedon. But the parish church, at least, remains as he would have known it, and the high coastal path, which passes the churchyard, still looks out on a startling prospect of 'Dim coasts, and cloud-like hills, and shoreless Ocean'.

Culbone

The coastal path to Culbone, memorably described by Dorothy Wordsworth in 1797, formerly led from the Worthy toll gate near Porlock Weir, and rose steeply through Yearnor Wood to the Exmoor high ground. Following a landslide in 1984 the path was abandoned, and an alternative route farther up the hillside is now also threatened. Access by road is from the A39 between Porlock and Lynton, or along the Worthy toll road from Porlock Weir.

Culbone's tiny church may be of Saxon origin and is set in great seclusion in Culbone Combe. Ash Farm stands a short distance south of the church and is usually identified as the place where 'Kubla Khan' was written. Coleridge probably knew the farm well, just as he also knew Broomstreet, two miles to the west. But the more likely setting for the composition of the poem was Withycombe Farm (now gone), which stood at a right-angle bend in the road a quarter of a mile south-east of Silcombe Farm.

Holford and Alfoxden

Holford, the gateway to the seaward slopes of the Quantock Hills, lies three miles west of Nether Stowey on the turnpike road to Williton. Alfoxden Park immediately adjoins the village, and Holford inevitably became a frequent part of the walks shared by Coleridge and the Wordsworths. They explored the two combes – Hodder's Combe and Holford Combe – which run south-west from the village; they walked to Woodlands, a mansion a short distance to the east; and they followed the Great Track from its beginning near the gate to Alfoxden Park, over Longstone Hill to West Quantoxhead.

On the western side of the village runs the heavily-wooded Holford Glen, now a reserve of the League Against Cruel Sports. A footbridge crosses the glen high above the place where the meeting of two Quantock streams forms a waterfall. This was once the 'loud Waterfall' described by Coleridge and Wordsworth, and though it is now considerably less impressive than it must once have been, it remains a powerfully evocative link with the events of 1797–8. So too does the lane on the farther side of the glen. It leads to Alfoxden, and can hardly have changed since Dorothy Wordsworth first described the oaks and hollies which grow profusely in the woodland bordering it. Alfoxden, which is reached after half a mile, is now a hotel. The right-of-way which passes the house can be followed either high into the Quantock Hills or down Pardlestone Lane to Putsham and Kilve.

Kilve

Wordsworth commemorated 'Kilve's delightful shore' in his poem 'Anecdote for Fathers', and Coleridge called Kilve beach 'our favorite seat'. It was there, according to Coleridge, that the government spy overheard a conversation in which he mistook 'Spinoza' for 'Spy Nozy' and concluded that his investigation of the poets had been discovered. Kilve church and chantry stand a short distance inland, and on the main road through the parish (the A39) is the hamlet of Putsham.

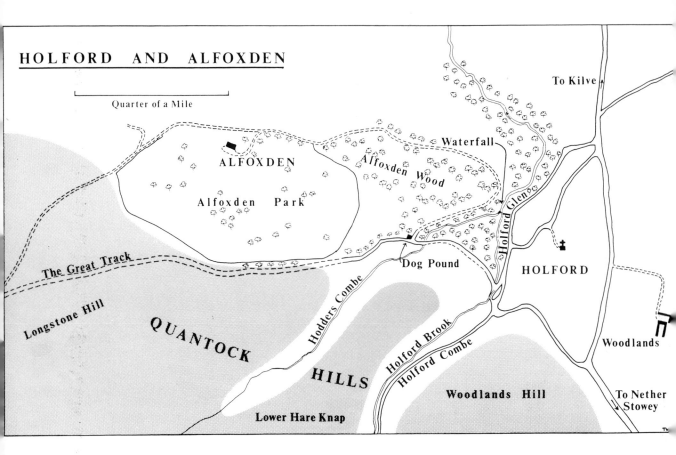

HOLFORD AND ALFOXDEN

Quarter of a Mile

John Bartholomew, tenant of the Alfoxden home farm, lived at Putsham farmhouse and was visited there by the Wordsworths.

Nether Stowey

Coleridge's Cottage at Nether Stowey stands at one end of Lime Street, the narrowest of Stowey's three main streets. In spite of much alteration during the nineteenth century, it is now clear that the cottage still possesses its three original ground-floor rooms and corresponding bed-chambers above. The cottage was acquired by the National Trust in 1909, and its two parlours are open to the public. Behind the cottage, in Coleridge's orchard, was the apple tree 'crook'd earthward' where Coleridge and Sara would sit together. Tom Poole's garden (now built over) adjoined the orchard at the back, and contained the celebrated lime-tree bower, described by Hazlitt as 'an arbour made of bark'.

Tom Poole's house (21 Castle Street) is an imposing eighteenth-century building in red sandstone. Its 'great windy parlour' has recently been restored, and Poole's vaulted bookroom survives at the back of the house. In about 1802 he moved to The Old House in St Mary Street. Although externally less impressive than his earlier home, he made of it a comfortable gentleman's residence, building for himself a finely-proportioned bookroom. Poole is buried beside his parents in the churchyard at Stowey, and a memorial to him is inside the church itself.

At the western end of Castle Street is the seventeenth century Castle Hill House. Coleridge's friend,

John Cruikshank, was tenant of the house in 1797, and presumably had his famous dream of a spectre ship while living there.

Over Stowey

The scattered parish of Over Stowey, which includes a large area of the Quantock Hills, was almost as well known to Coleridge as its more flourishing neighbour, Nether Stowey. At Marshmills, a substantial house on the road from Nether Stowey to Plainsfield, Coleridge first met Tom Poole's disapproving cousins, and in the hamlet of Adscombe was the cottage (unidentified) in which he had originally hoped to settle. The surviving ruins of Adscombe Chapel, a building commemorated in 'The Foster-Mother's Tale', were finally demolished in 1964.

Shurton

Shurton, a hamlet in Stogursey parish, lies three miles north of Nether Stowey. It has a significant place in Coleridge's history, since it was on a visit to his Cambridge contemporary, Henry Poole of Shurton Court, that Coleridge first discovered both Nether Stowey and Tom Poole. Shurton Court, recently restored, stands in a walled garden off Shurton Lane. North of the house, a track crosses the fields to Shurton Bars, the coastal area a mile from the hamlet which was to be the setting for Coleridge's poem 'Lines Written at Shurton Bars'. Only the looming presence of Hinkley Point Power Station mars the beauty of the scene.

Taunton

During the period that Coleridge lived in Nether Stowey, he frequently made the journey over the Quantock Hills to Taunton, where he preached for Dr Joshua Toulmin, the town's much-persecuted Unitarian minister. The Unitarian chapel stands in Mary Street, and survives in fine completeness behind an undistinguished façade. The chapel was opened in 1721 and possesses one of the best-preserved interiors of any Nonconformist church in the West Country. The black oak pulpit from which Coleridge preached is carved with acanthus, vines, and grapes, and the pulpit Bible of 1715 is the same that he would have used.

Watchet

Coleridge and the Wordsworths probably stayed the night at Watchet during the walking tour which gave rise to 'The Ancient Mariner'. The Bell Inn, where tradition says the first of the poem was committed to writing, survives in Market Street. The harbour close by was probably the original of the harbour from which the mariner set sail.

NOTES AND REFERENCES

ABBREVIATIONS USED
(Place of publication is London, unless otherwise stated)

Biographia   Samuel Taylor Coleridge, *Biographia Literaria*, ed. James Engell and W. Jackson Bate (2 vols, 1983)

Campbell   James Dykes Campbell, *Samuel Taylor Coleridge: a Narrative of the Events of his Life* (1896)

CL   *Collected Letters of Samuel Taylor Coleridge*, ed. Earl Leslie Griggs (6 vols, Oxford, 1956–71)

Collinson   John Collinson, *The History and Antiquities of the County of Somerset* (3 vols, Bath, 1791; supplement, Taunton, 1939)

Cottle   Joseph Cottle, *Reminiscences of Samuel Taylor Coleridge and Robert Southey* (1847)

Crosse   Mrs Andrew Crosse, *Red-Letter Days of My Life* (2 vols, 1892)

De Quincey   Thomas De Quincey, *Recollections of the Lakes and the Lake Poets*, ed. David Wright (1970)

DNB   *The Dictionary of National Biography* (1885–)

Evans and Pinney   Bergen Evans and Hester Pinney, 'Racedown and the Wordsworths', *Review of English Studies*, VIII (1932), 1–18

EY   *The Letters of William and Dorothy Wordsworth: the Early Years 1787–1805*, ed. Ernest de Selincourt, revised Chester L. Shaver (Oxford, 1967)

Gillman   James Gillman, *The Life of Samuel Taylor Coleridge* (1838)

Grosart   *The Prose Works of William Wordsworth*, ed. Alexander B Grosart (3 vols, 1876)

Hazlitt   William Hazlitt, *Selected Writings*, ed. Ronald Blythe (1970)

Holland   *Paupers and Pig Killers: the Diary of William Holland, a Somerset Parson, 1799–1818*, ed. Jack Ayres (Gloucester, 1984)

Knight, 1889   William Knight, *The Life of William Wordsworth* (2 vols, Edinburgh, 1889)

Knight, 1897   *Journals of Dorothy Wordsworth*, ed. William Knight (2 vols, 1897)

Moorman   *Journals of Dorothy Wordsworth*, ed. Mary Moorman (Oxford, 1971)

Lamb   Charles Lamb, *Elia and the Last Essays of Elia*, ed. Jonathan Bate (Oxford, 1987)

LCL   *The Letters of Charles and Mary Lamb*, ed. Edwin J. Marrs Jr (3 vols, continuing, Ithaca, 1975–)

Lefebure   Molly Lefebure, *The Bondage of Love: a Life of Mrs Samuel Taylor Coleridge* (1986)

LY   *The Letters of William and Dorothy Wordsworth: the Later Years 1821–1853*, ed. Ernest de Selincourt, revised Alan G. Hill (4 vols, Oxford, 1978–88)

MAT   *Minnow Among Tritons: Mrs. S.T. Coleridge's Letters to Thomas Poole, 1799–1834*, ed. Stephen Potter (1934)

Native Home   John A. Whitham, *My Native Home: Samuel Taylor Coleridge of Ottery St Mary, Devon* (Ottery St Mary, 1984)

Nichols   William L. Nichols, *The Quantocks and their Associations* (2nd ed. 1891)

NLRS   *New Letters of Robert Southey*, ed. Kenneth Curry (2 vols, New York, 1965)

Notebooks	*The Notebooks of Samuel Taylor Coleridge*, ed. Kathleen Coburn (3 double vols, continuing, 1957–)
Ottery St Mary	John A. Whitham, *Ottery St Mary: a Devonshire Town* (Chichester, 1984)
Pares	Richard Pares, *A West-India Fortune* (1950)
Poole	Mrs Henry Sandford, *Thomas Poole and his Friends* (2 vols, 1888)
Prelude	William Wordsworth, *The Prelude, or Growth of a Poet's Mind (Text of 1805)*, ed. Ernest de Selincourt, corrected Stephen Gill (Oxford, 1970)
PW	*Coleridge: Poetical Works*, ed. Ernest Hartley Coleridge (Oxford, 1912)
Roe	Nicholas Roe, *Wordsworth and Coleridge: the Radical Years* (Oxford, 1988)
Southey	*The Life and Correspondence of Robert Southey*, ed. Charles Cuthbert Southey (6 vols, 1849–50)
SRO	Somerset Record Office, Taunton
Table Talk	*The Table Talk and Omniana of Samuel Taylor Coleridge*, ed. Coventry Patmore (Oxford, 1917)
Transactions	*Transactions of the Exeter Diocesan Architectural Society*, I (Exeter, 1843)
VCH	*The Victoria History of the Counties of England: a History of the County of Somerset*, V, ed. R.W. Dunning (Oxford, 1985)
Watchman	Samuel Taylor Coleridge, *The Watchman*, ed. Lewis Patton (1970)
Whalley	George Whalley, 'Coleridge and Southey in Bristol, 1795', *Review of English Studies*, New Series I (1950), 324–40

PREFACE
1 *CL*, I, 397

INTRODUCTION
1 *CL*, I, 217–18
2 *CL*, I, 227
3 *PW*, 263
4 The earlier spelling 'Alfoxden' has been used throughout the book in preference to the modern 'Alfoxton'.

CHAPTER 1: 'VISIONS OF CHILDHOOD'
1 *PW*, 48; William Marshall, *The Rural Economy of the West of England* (2 vols, 1796), II, 110; *Ottery St Mary*, 55–6
2 *Ottery St Mary*, 12; *DNB*: 'Grandison, John'; *Transactions*, 7–9
3 *Transactions*, 98
4 Ibid., 42–3, 48; *CL*, I, 311
5 Lord Coleridge, KC, *The Story of a Devonshire House* (1905), *passim*; genealogical papers of A.H.B. Coleridge, held by Lord Coleridge. Family tradition says that Coleridge used the phrase from *Macbeth* to a nephew who was 'getting above himself'.
6 Genealogical papers of A.H.B. Coleridge; Devon Record Office: Throwleigh parish records; *CL*, I, 302–3, 528; *Native Home*, 1.
7 *Devon and Cornwall Notes and Queries*, IX (1916–17), 217
8 *CL*, I, 302, 310; De Quincey, 58
9 *CL*, I, 311
10 Ibid., 347–8; *PW*, 40, 54
11 *CL*, I, 347, 354; *Ottery St Mary*, 38
12 *CL*, I, 312, 348
13 Ibid., 348, 352–3
14 *Notebooks*, I, entry 1416; *CL*, I, 353–4
15 *CL*, I, 355
16 Ibid., 387–8; *Native Home*, 12–13

17 *CL*, I, 1; *PW*, 11–12, 48, 242; *Prelude*, VI, 274–84
18 *Calendar of Patent Rolls, Edward IV*, V (1926), 283; *Table Talk*, 198; *CL*, I, 388–9; Lamb,17
19 Gillman, 17
20 Lamb, 15
21 Gillman, 17, 20; *CL*, I, 260
22 *Biographia*, I, 8–11
23 Lamb, 24–5
24 *PW*, 11; Gillman, 23; *Table Talk*, 102–3; *Biographia*, 13–15
25 *CL*, V, 218
26 *CL*, I, 15–17, 31, 34, 45
27 Ibid., 36–8
28 Ibid., 53
29 Ibid., 49, 68
30 Ibid., 61n
31 Ibid., 62–4, 75–6
32 Ibid., 67, 80

CHAPTER 2: 'EPIDEMIC DELUSION'
 1 *CL*, I, 82; *Prelude*, XIII, 1–65
 2 *CL*, I, 82; *PW*, 174; *CL*, II, 959
 3 Lefebure, 26–7; *NLRS*, I, 36
 4 *NLRS*, I, 56, 61
 5 *Poole*, I, 96–9
 6 *CL*, I, 82–3, 90
 7 Ibid., 87–9, 92
 8 Ibid., 96; Campbell, 31; *NLRS*, I, 64, 67, 75; *DNB*: 'Lovell, Robert'
 9 Lefebure, 41; Cottle, 5–6
10 *NLRS*, I, 68; *DNB*: 'Southey, Robert'; Collinson, supplement, 70
11 *NLRS*, I, 68; Lefebure, 41
12 *NLRS*, I, 68–9; Collinson, II, 126; *PW*, 58–9
13 *NLRS*, I, 68–9
14 *CL*, I, 88; *NLRS*, I, 69; Collinson, III, 574
15 SRO: D/D/Rt 164; *Charles Lamb Bulletin*, New Series XX (Oct. 1977), 69–72; *DNB*: 'Burnett, George'
16 J.A. Venn, *Alumni Cantabrigienses*, V (Cambridge, 1953): 'Poole, Henry'
17 *Poole*, I, 176; *PW*, 252
18 *VCH*, V, 196
19 SRO: Q/REl 41/33
20 *Poole*, I, 24
21 De Quincey, 35; *VCH*,V, 195; *Poole*, I, 7, 9
22 *Poole*, I, 20–1, 23, 92
23 Ibid., 96–9
24 Ibid., 12
25 Ibid., 103–4
26 Ibid., 101; *Holland*, 22; Crosse, I, 7–9
27 Campbell, 31; Lefebure, 41–2; *NLRS*, I, 71. Evidence for the date and place of Coleridge's proposal of marriage is better than is usually suggested. Southey clearly says that the proposal was made at his mother's house in Bath after the Somerset tour, and the matter was evidently settled by the time he began a letter to Horace Walpole Bedford on 22 August.
28 Campbell, 31
29 *NLRS*, I, 71, 74

CHAPTER 3: BRISTOL AND CLEVEDON

1   *CL*, I,103
2   Ibid., 119
3   Ibid., 105, 107, 112–13
4   *NLRS*, I, 82–3
5   *CL*, I, 130, 144
6   Ibid., 145; Cottle, 405–6; *NLRS*, 90–2
7   *CL*, I, 150; Whalley, 339n
8   *CL*, I, 152; Cottle, 13–14, 17–18, 406
9   Robert Woof, 'Wordsworth and Coleridge: Some Early Matters', in *Bicentenary Wordsworth Studies*, ed. Jonathan Wordsworth (Ithaca, 1970), 76–91; *EY*, 153
10   *CL*, I, 151; De Quincey, 53
11   *CL*, I, 163–73; Cottle, 27–35
12   *Poole*, I, 128; *CL*, I, 170
13   *PW*, 100, 106; Cottle, 41; *CL*, I, 158
14   *CL*, I, 167; *Poole*, 117, 124–6
15   *PW*, 94, 96–100; *Holland*, 41, 69
16   Cottle, 40; *CL*, I, 160; Lefebure, 72–3
17   *CL*, I, 159–60; Cottle, 41–2
18   *PW*, 101; Cottle, 39
19   Cottle, 64; *PW*, 107
20   *Watchman*, xxviii–xxix
21   *CL*, I, 152n; Cottle, 74–6; *Biographia*, I, 179; *Watchman*, xxxii
22   *CL*, I, 178–9
23   *Biographia*, I, 180
24   *CL*, I, 188–9; Cottle, 78
25   *Watchman*, lv; *CL*, I, 208; Cottle, 83
26   *CL*, I, 193, 207–8, 211–12; *Poole*, I, 146; *CL*, I, 204
27   *Poole*, I, 143–4; *CL*, I, 209–10, 217
28   *CL*, I, 222, 227, 234, 237, 240

CHAPTER 4: 'A BEAUTIFUL COUNTRY'

1   *CL*, I, 249
2   Ibid., 237, 240, 255; *PW*, 154
3   *CL*, I, 273–4
4   *PW*, 183; *CL*, I, 240, 242, 250–1
5   *CL*, I, 263, 269, 272–3
6   Ibid., 277, 288, 292
7   *Holland*, 136, 163, 170; *PW*, 168
8   SRO: DD/V; *CL*, I, 288, 436; *MAT*, 175; *CL*, I, 296, 301, 308
9   *CL*, I, 301; *Biographia*, I, 188; *CL*, I, 204, 643; *Poole*, I, 111; *CL*, I, 572
10   *CL*, I, 297, 308, 481
11   *Biographia*, I, 195–6; *Notebooks*, I, entries 213, 217
12   *CL*, I, 304, 318; *PW*, 173–4
13   *CL*, I, 301n, 315–16
14   Ibid., 320n, 321
15   Ibid., 319n, 320, 325
16   *CL*, I, 323–4; Cottle, 116; *CL*, I, 301, 326
17   James Gibson (ed.), *The Complete Poems of Thomas Hardy* (1976), 320; George R. Pulman, *Book of the Axe* (1875), 193
18   For Racedown and the Pinneys *see* Pares, and Evans and Pinney
19   *EY*, 5, 281

20 *Prelude*, X, 900, 904–20
21 Pares, 142–3; Evans and Pinney, 9; *EY*, 147, 160, 166, 180
22 *EY*, 161–2, 169, 181
23 Ibid., 169, 186; Evans and Pinney, 17–18; *LY*, IV, 719

CHAPTER 5: 'WORDSWORTH & HIS EXQUISITE SISTER'
 1 *LY*, IV, 719; *CL*, II, 1060; *CL*, I, 326
 2 *EY*, 189; *CL*, I, 325–7; Christopher Wordsworth, *Memoirs of William Wordsworth* (1851), II, 288–90
 3 *EY*, 188–9
 4 *CL*, I, 328–9, 336
 5 Ibid., 330–1
 6 De Quincey, 53; *CL*, I, 331, 334
 7 Grosart, III, 159; *EY*, 190
 8 Collinson, I, 264; *VCH*, V, 3; *Burke's Landed Gentry* (1858): 'St Albyn of Alfoxton'; *EY*, 190
 9 *CL*, I, 330n; *LCL*, I, 224; *PW*, 179
10 *CL*, I, 266; *Poole*, I, 225–6
11 *CL*, I, 334; *EY*, 190
12 *EY*, 191
13 *CL*, I, 336; *LCL*, I, 117; Roe, 261
14 *CL*, I, 339; *Table Talk*, 122, and cf. Grosart, III, 20
15 *CL*, I, 332; Roe, 261; *Poole*, I, 235
16 Cottle, 181; Roe, 252
17 For the 'Spy Nozy' incident *see* Roe, 248–62, which supersedes all other accounts.
18 *Holland*, 41
19 *Biographia*, I, 193–4; *Holland*, 142, 158, 193
20 *Biographia*, I, 195
21 *CL*, I, 343
22 *Idem*; *Notebooks*, III, entry 4006; *CL*, I, 349–50
23 Collinson, II, 4
24 F.W. Weaver, *Somerset Medieval Wills* (Somerset Record Society, XXI) (1905), 13; Raymond Lister, *The Paintings of Samuel Palmer* (1985), plate 34
25 *Notebooks*, III, entry 4006 (notes). It is not true, as is sometimes stated, that 'Brimson' is or was a local pronunciation of 'Broomstreet'. [Information of Colin Sage.]
26 *CL*, I, 350
27 *PW*, 296
28 When the large Alfoxden library was sold in 1894, it included 'Travels of Anacharsis, 17 vols . . . 1741', 'Townsend's Conquest of Mexico, 1724', 'Harris's Voyages, 2 vols., 1705', and 'Ramsay's Travels of Cyrus, 2 vols., 1728'; it also contained an edition of Coleridge's poems, but nothing by Wordsworth (SRO: DD/SCL 24).

CHAPTER 6: *LYRICAL BALLADS*
 1 *CL*, I, 355–6
 2 Ibid., 346–8, 352–5
 3 *Poole*, II, 234–7; Nichols, 39–47
 4 Nichols, 40–1
 5 *EY*, 194; *PW*, 285–7
 6 *EY*, 194; Grosart, III, 17; *Poole*, I, 247
 7 Grosart, III, 17; 'Notes and Queries', *Somerset County Herald*, 2 Dec. 1944
 8 *CL*, I, 357
 9 *Table Talk*, 425; *EY*, 194
10 *CL*, I, 361, 366

11 Ibid., 362–3, 367
12 Ibid., 369–70
13 Hazlitt, 43–55
14 *CL*, I, 374, 380–1
15 Appendix I, 158
16 Robert Gittings (ed.), *Letters of John Keats* (1987), 157; *CL*, I, 330–1; Appendix I, 158–9
17 *Biographia*, I, 194; Appendix I, 159
18 Appendix I, 162
19 *EY*, 213; *CL*, I, 402
20 *CL*, I, 399–400; *Biographia*, II, 5–7
21 *EY*, 200
22 Grosart, III, 25–7, 41, 160
23 *Notebooks*, III, entry 4006; *CL*, I, 403–5
24 Hazlitt, 55–65
25 *CL*, I, 407
26 Grosart, III, 158
27 Cottle, 178; *CL*, I, 412; *EY*, 219
28 *EY*, 223
29 *Idem*
30 Grosart, III, 45
31 *CL*, I, 415
32 Ibid., 416

CHAPTER 7: 'I FEEL WHAT I HAVE LOST'
 1 *CL*, I, 416
 2 *Poole*, I, 278; *CL*, I, 449
 3 Lefebure, 105–9
 4 *Poole*, I, 291; *MAT*, 1–3
 5 *Poole*, I, 219; *CL*, I, 479, 484
 6 *CL*, I, 523; Lefebure, 122
 7 *CL*, I, 528
 8 Campbell, 104
 9 *CL*, I, 530, 533–4, 542n
10 Ibid., 537, 540
11 Ibid., 542n
12 Ibid., 543n, 544–5
13 Ibid., 545n, 547, 558
14 Ibid., 481, 572; *Poole*, II, 8; *CL*, I, 562, 575, 582
15 Lefebure, 127; *CL*, I, 608
16 *Poole*, II, 23–4; *CL*, I, 584, 643
17 *CL*, I, 778, 780, 787
18 Ibid., 789–98; Moorman, 105; *PW*, 362–8
19 *CL*, II, 926–7
20 *PW*, 403–8; *Prelude*, XIII, 386–96
21 Lefebure, 183–4
22 *MAT*, 10; *Poole*, II, 184; *CL*, III, 29
23 *Notebooks*, II, entry 3170; De Quincey, 42
24 De Quincey, 33–56
25 *Notebooks*, II, entry 3128; *CL*, III, 24
26 *Notebooks*, II, entry 3148
27 Ibid., entry 2557
28 *CL*, III, 459n

29 Ibid., 462–4
30 Ibid., 490, 542
31 Campbell, 259; *Poole*, II, 294
32 Campbell, 278
33 Whalley, 33; Cottle, 410–11; *Southey*, VI, 310
34 *Southey*, VI, 316, 318; Cottle, 411, 418–19
35 *LY*, IV, 189–202
36 Grosart, II, 159–60; *LY*, IV, 198n
37 *LY*, IV, 200n; *Ottery St Mary*, 71
38 *Poems by Hartley Coleridge, with a Memoir by his Brother* (2 vols, 1851), I, xxii, lix, clxxxv
39 Crosse, I, 5, 7–9

APPENDIX I: DOROTHY WORDSWORTH'S ALFOXDEN JOURNAL, 1798

1 Dorothy Wordsworth's Alfoxden journal was first published in incomplete form by Professor William Knight in Knight, 1889, and was given in a fuller, though still not quite complete, version in Knight, 1897. At an unknown date between 1897 and 1940 the manuscript was lost, and all twentieth-century editions have hitherto relied on Knight, 1897. In the text given here, his two versions have been collated, and it has been possible as a result to restore a few original spellings and some lost words. The lighter punctuation used in the version of 1889 has generally been followed, though much of the remaining punctuation is likely to be editorial none the less: in particular, most of the abundant semi-colons were probably introduced by Knight to replace Dorothy Wordsworth's characteristic dashes.

2 The semi-colon supplied here follows Moorman, 1.

3 The village of Holford lies three-quarters of a mile east of Alfoxden. The house and park at Alfoxden formed a detached part of Stringston parish, to the north-east, and it was in Stringston Church that the St Albyn family, owners of the house, were traditionally buried.

4 When referring in the journal to the 'larger' and the 'smaller' combes, Dorothy Wordsworth was probably distinguishing between Holford Combe and Hodder's Combe. They run on either side of Lower Hare Knap, a short distance from Alfoxden.

5 The 'manufacturer' may have been a silk weaver, the remains of whose house survive in Holford Glen, next to Holford brook.

6 Perhaps the mill at Kilve.

7 Hollies still grow plentifully beneath the oaks and beeches along the lane to Alfoxden.

8 The Castle of Comfort, on the road from Holford to Nether Stowey, was 'a kind of Pot House'. The landlord, John Mogg, had a large bottle-nose which Coleridge may have attributed, for comic effect, to the spy who came to Nether Stowey in 1797 (*see above*, p. 98).

9 John Bartholomew (pronounced 'Bartelmy') lived at Putsham Farm in Kilve. He was the tenant of Alfoxden, and sub-let the house to the Wordsworths.

10 Knight, 1897 omits 'gaunt . . . lamb'.

11 Entries for 3–5 February are misdated: Coleridge was staying with the Wedgwood brothers at Cote House, Westbury-on-Trym, on these days. *See* Moorman, 4n.

12 Flat Holm and Steep Holm in the Bristol Channel.

13 A hamlet in Holford parish consisting chiefly of Woodlands Farm and Woodlands House. Close to the farm, until 1912, stood a beech tree traditionally identified as the 'trysting place' of Coleridge and the Wordsworths. The house is a mansion of *c.* 1790, later occupied by John Kenyon, the friend of Robert and Elizabeth Barrett Browning. Coleridge briefly thought of living there after leaving the cottage at Nether Stowey (*CL*, I, 455).

14 They were birch trees.

15 'Potsdam' was Dorothy Wordsworth's spelling of Putsham, a hamlet in Kilve parish on the turnpike road from Nether Stowey to Minehead. It was easily reached from Alfoxden down the supposedly-haunted Pardlestone Lane.

16 Marks of ellipsis here and below indicate Knight's omissions.

17   The waterfall was in Holford Glen, half a mile from Alfoxden.

18   Coleridge and the Wordsworths called Holford Glen 'the dell'.

19   Basil Montagu, the younger, the child of Basil Montagu, the elder, lived with the Wordsworths at Racedown and Alfoxden, 1795–8.

20   Knight, 1889, has 'the fresh-ploughed fields dark'.

21   John Cruikshank was the son of William Cruikshank, the agent for Lord Egmont of Enmore Castle. John Cruikshank rented Castle Hill House, Nether Stowey, and it was probably there that he had the dream of a spectre ship which inspired 'The Ancient Mariner'.

22   The Iron Age hill-fort called Dowsborough or Danesborough to the east of Holford Combe. It occupies one of the highest points of the Quantock Hills.

23   Indicates Knight's omission, both here and below.

24   Cf. 'Christabel', ll. 49–50: 'The one red leaf, the last of its clan, / That dances as often as dance it can . . .'

25   Possibly Christopher Tricky, the inspiration for Wordsworth's poem 'Simon Lee, the Old Huntsman'. *See above*, pp. 96–7.

26   Moorman, 10n, suggests that Charles Lloyd is meant.

27   *See* Wordsworth's poem, 'A whirl-blast from behind the hill'.

28   The stunted thorn and the muddy pond beside it inspired Wordsworth's poem, 'The Thorn'.

29   Presumably 'The Ancient Mariner'. The expression 'the horned moon', used in this entry and that for 21 March, echoes ll. 210–11 of the poem: 'The hornéd Moon, with one bright star / Within the nether tip.'

30   Copper mines were opened at Dodington in 1784 by the Marquis of Buckingham. *See* J.R. Hamilton and J.F. Lawrence, *Men and Mining on the Quantocks* (Bracknell, 1970).

31   The Chesters were a farming family who lived originally at Dodington Hall. By the time Coleridge and the Wordsworths knew them, they had moved to Nether Stowey. John Chester accompanied Coleridge to Germany in September 1798. *See* Berta Lawrence, *Coleridge and Wordsworth in Somerset* (Newton Abbot, 1970), 135–40.

32   Cf. 'Christabel', l. 22.

33   Thomas Wedgwood (1771–1805), son of the potter, who with his brother Josiah gave Coleridge an annuity of £150 a year in January 1798.

34   The uncharacteristically brief entries for 28 March–1 April may reflect Dorothy Wordsworth's distress at her part in Coleridge's growing quarrel with Charles Lloyd. *See* Robert Gittings and Jo Manton, *Dorothy Wordsworth* (Oxford, 1985), 81.

35   'Crookham' is Crowcombe on the southern flanks of the Quantocks. The appeal, against Land Tax, was evidently successful: Wordsworth's name does not appear in the Land Tax assessments.

36   Moorman, 13n, demonstrates that the references in this entry should be to 'Mrs Coleridge'. Coleridge was in Ottery St Mary at the time.

37   Crowcombe Court, built 1724–39 by Thomas Carew, was given its picturesque grounds in the 1770s by James Bernard, Carew's son-in-law. A folly in the form of a ruined gothic chapel survives.

38   Lower Hare Knap.

39   The picture, the earliest of Wordsworth that is known, was by W. Shuter. The same artist also painted Coleridge's portrait.

40   The entry is misdated: 22 May was a Tuesday.

41   Cross, a hamlet in the parish of Compton Bishop, contained a well-known coaching inn.

PICTURE CREDITS

INDEX

C = Samuel Taylor Coleridge; W = William Wordsworth. Page numbers in *italics* refer to illustrations. For places marked with an asterisk see also Appendix II.